PERLY'S RESTAURANT AND DELICATESSEN SHOT BY MOLLY PETERSON

METZGER BAR & BUTCHERY SHOT BY MARCELLA LEE

Copyright © 2015, Blunt Objects, LLC

All rights reserved. No part of this book may be reproduced or transmitted in any portion, form or fashion, without permission from the publisher.

Published by Blunt Objects, LLC, Oilville, Virginia
Acquisitions Editor | Carrie Fleck Walters
For permissions, contact carrie@blunt-objects.com.
http://blunt-objects.com | http://804ork.com
Printed in China.

804ork Vol. 2 | Back for Seconds
by Kim Catley, Chris Gatewood, Marcella Lee, Carrie Walters
Includes index.
ISBN 978-0-692-46203-4

VOL. 2

80

BACK FOR SECONDS

A SERIES OF COOKBOOKS FEATURING **RICHMOND'S** MOST ADMIRED **CHEFS, RESTAURANTS,** AND **CUISINE**

CREATIVE TEAM
KIM CATLEY
CHRIS GATEWOOD
MARCELLA LEE
CARRIE WALTERS

PHOTOGRAPHERS
CHRISTOPHILE KONSTAS
MARCELLA LEE
MOLLY PETERSON
KIERAN WAGNER

PUBLISHED BY
BLUNT OBJECTS
OILVILLE, VIRGINIA

THE DAILY KITCHEN AND BAR SHOT BY MOLLY PETERSON

THE DOG AND PIG SHOW SHOT BY MARCELLA LEE

MENU

SERVED DAILY

breakfast, lunch, dinner & late night

804ORK

VOLUME 2: BACK FOR SECONDS

FOREWORD

PAGE 5

LAURA SANT
Saveur

EDITOR'S NOTE

PAGE 7

CARRIE WALTERS
Blunt Objects

---

chapter ONE — THE SPECIALISTS — 8

10
BOMBOLINI PASTA
JOHN KRECKMAN

16
EARLY BIRD BISCUIT CO. & BAKERY
TIM LAXTON

22
PIZZA TONIGHT
VICTORIA DEROCHE

28
SHORYUKEN RAMEN
WILL RICHARDSON

chapter TWO — NEW AMERICAN — 36

38
TARRANT'S CAFÉ
TED SANTARELLA

46
THE SAVORY GRAIN
SEAN MURPHY & JAMI BOHDAN

58
BOKA GRILL AND GROWLERS
PATRICK HARRIS

68
THE DAILY KITCHEN AND BAR
MICHELLE WILLIAMS

chapter THREE — NEIGHBORHOOD EATS — 80

82
THE CONTINENTAL WESTHAMPTON
STUART LOWRIE

92
THE DOG AND PIG SHOW
ISABEL & JAMES ECKROSH

98
CROAKER'S SPOT
NEVERETT EGGLESTON III

106
LUNCH. AND SUPPER!
RICK LYONS

114
PERLY'S RESTAURANT AND DELICATESSEN
RACHELLE & KEVIN ROBERTS

chapter FOUR — TASTES FROM ABROAD — 124

126
GRAFFIATO RICHMOND
MIKE ISABELLA & MATT ROBINETT

136
METZGER BAR & BUTCHERY
BRITTANNY ANDERSON

146
DECO RISTORANTE
GIUSEPPE SCAFIDI

154
SAISON
ADAM HALL

chapter FIVE — OUT OF THE ORDINARY — 164

166
SOUTHBOUND
JOE SPARATTA & LEE GREGORY

178
THE URBAN TAVERN
TIM BEREIKA

188
THE ROGUE GENTLEMEN
JOHN MAHER

198
L'OPOSSUM
DAVID SHANNON

CONTRIBUTORS

PHOTOGRAPHERS 210 | CREATIVE TEAM 212 | ACKNOWLEDGMENTS 214

DIRECTORY 216

INDEX 218

— FOREWORD —

RICHMOND, VIRGINIA

RICHMOND 1864

— FOREWORD —

LAURA SANT

EDITOR | SAVEUR

In the months before I moved away from Richmond, my friends and I devised something we called the Alphabet Tour: We would eat at a Richmond restaurant that began with each letter of the alphabet in order, starting with A and working all the way to Z. If we did two a week, we'd make it through 26 places before I left: A nice farewell. The project started a lot of arguments: Was Comfort or Can Can the more deserving pick for C? Should Mamma Zu count for Z, or was that cheating? Should we prioritize places we'd never been before, or should it be a tour of our old favorites? If the choice of restaurant ended in a stalemate, who got the final vote?

We only managed to make it through the letter E (Edo's Squid; a unanimous decision) before I left, but I believe it says a lot that my main concern before leaving the city was whether or not I'd get to eat at enough of its restaurants. Those of us who have lived in Richmond know: The food has always been good.

If back then you had to know your way around to get to the really good spots, now it seems you can't walk 10 feet—or open the pages of a magazine—without stumbling on a fantastic new restaurant. Over the years I've watched Richmond go from somewhere I felt I needed to talk up or explain to people (*no really, the food is great!*) to a place that's regularly lauded in the national media for its food scene. It's become a culinary destination in its own right, recognized both for the spots that have been there for decades as well as the wave of innovative newcomers that have set up shop in the city, having recognized a good thing when they saw it. It's now common knowledge that Richmond is a place to go not just for really good Southern food, but also for incredible Greek cuisine, Sichuan meals, Liberian-inspired food, and creative New American dishes. The James Beard Foundation honored Sally Bell's Kitchen with an America's Classics Award this year; Colman Andrews declared Richmond "the next great American food city" in *Departures* magazine in August of 2014; and the late Josh Ozersky called out two beloved Richmond spots—Sub Rosa bakery and Rappahannock—when he declared Virginia the "food region of 2014." Richmond even has its own food festival now—Fire, Flour & Fork—that draws chefs, food writers, bartenders, producers, and food lovers from all over the country. When Sarah Simmons, chef-owner of New York City's Birds & Bubbles and CITY GRIT, visited Richmond, she said that, "what started as a quick visit to see our friends turned into a long weekend of eating our way through a town we've never considered to be a 'dining destination.' We didn't have one morsel of food we didn't love, from some of the most authentic Greek food to Chinese dishes rivaling anything served in Flushing."

Each time I return to Richmond, I'm surprised by the sheer number of fantastic restaurants that have appeared since my last visit. There's never enough time—or room in my stomach—to try them all. And yet what impresses me the most is that as the restaurant and bar scene continues to grow at an astonishing speed, the small-town community feel remains. There's some healthy competition, yes, but overall the feeling is one of collaboration, support, and camaraderie.

It fills me with pride—and a touch of homesickness—to watch all this happen from afar. To meet chefs and food writers and have them wax poetic about the city you consider your own is a little bit like having everyone suddenly discover the under-the-radar band you've loved for years; you're thrilled, but a small part of you is sad that it's no longer your little secret.

It's a very small part, though, because it's incredibly gratifying to watch the city I'll always consider my home finally get its due. And if that makes it harder to get into Saison or score an Early Bird biscuit in the morning, I'm OK with that. I'll be over here with my ever-growing list of places to try, watching the restaurant scene in Richmond continue to inspire people all over the country. I can't wait to see what recipes I'll be cooking—and from which yet-to-be-opened incredible places—in *804ork Volume 10*.

— A NOTE FROM THE EDITOR —

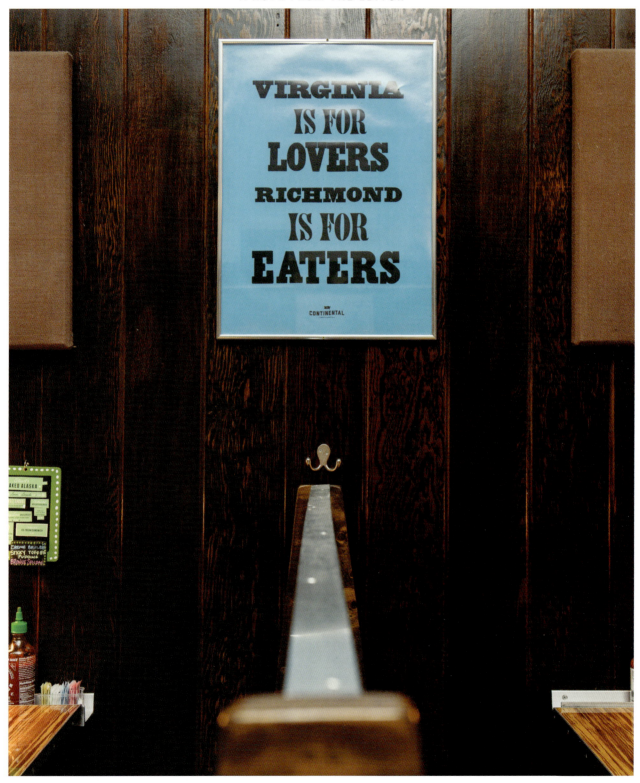

— A NOTE FROM THE EDITOR —

BACK FOR SECONDS

CARRIE WALTERS

TWENTY-ONE RESTAURANTS

TWENTY-SIX OWNERS & CHEFS

FIFTY-SIX BRAND-NEW RECIPES

Not long after *804ork* hit the shelves I Instagrammed a shot of this poster (most likely while I anxiously awaited the world's best BLT and contemplated whether or not it was OK to order Baked Alaska in the middle of the day). This statement, casually hung over a booth at The Continental Westhampton, brought up a feeling of pride. Not in a gross *we're all training for a cable TV eating competition show and can't wait to become America's unhealthiest city* kind of a way—but a *hell yes our city loves its food and we're not kidding around so you better respect* kind of a way. Judging by the response I got, others agree.

I have a tendency to get really into research and become a little too focused on specific topics when I'm working on a project. When I started *804ork* at the end of 2012, I thought I was just picking up on a lot of food talk because I was looking for it. Like that time I discovered the alarmingly high rate of surgical fires while working on an ER campaign. I digress.

This time it wasn't just me. Everyone *really was* talking about food. Our Thursday night mainstays were popping up in *GQ* and being hat-tipped by Alton Brown. The people who so graciously helped out with our little cookbook were being nominated for James Beard awards. Speaking of that lil' old cookbook, *Saveur* even went so far as declaring it *worth buying*!

But here's the thing: We don't need people to tell us what we already know. It's great the rest of the world is finally catching on, but that doesn't change this city and the amazing meals within.

"Are you going to do another cookbook?!"

I got that question a lot. The truth is, the first book was a ton of work and it wasn't always fun. So maybe it was the energy brought on by all the talk, and the vision of this poster tucked away in my mind, or the fact I really just love looking at beautiful pictures of food—but I couldn't walk away from a project that represented so much.

So here we are at Volume 2. Naturally we wanted to make this book even better. To do so we dug a little deeper into the stories behind the chefs and restaurants, and even went behind-the-scenes to show step-by-step instructions and details for some of the more complex recipes. Because I like to make things difficult, I redesigned the format, keeping the recipes together with the restaurant's profile and grouping them into chapters by theme. We also brought on a recipe editor to make sure the recipes were accurate and more friendly for the home chef. Ultimately we think this volume will be more fun to read and much easier to use.

Like the original, we also hope that this edition properly captures a snapshot of the current food scene and highlights some of your favorite—or soon-to-be favorite—spots and dishes.

Happy reading and—more importantly—eating!

CHAPTER ONE
THE SPECIALISTS

4 CHEFS

5 RECIPES

Do one thing, and do it well. It's advice we all have heard and to these four chefs, it's advice that's been taken to heart. So much so that one thing even has permanent placement on the front of their door—biscuits, pasta, pizza, ramen. That's a pretty big commitment to a flagship dish.

As these chefs can tell you, a narrow focus can build a wide following. Small beginnings and a limited but focused menu have put them on the map. So while they are likely to add to their offerings over time (as some already have), we know and can expect that they will keep those namesake dishes coming.

We decided we'd begin this volume of 804rk with a collection of Richmond's perfectionists—turning seemingly simple ingredients into mainstay masterpieces that we find ourselves going back for again and again. And again.

— CHAPTER ONE: THE SPECIALISTS —

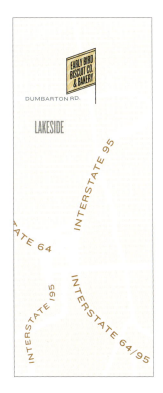

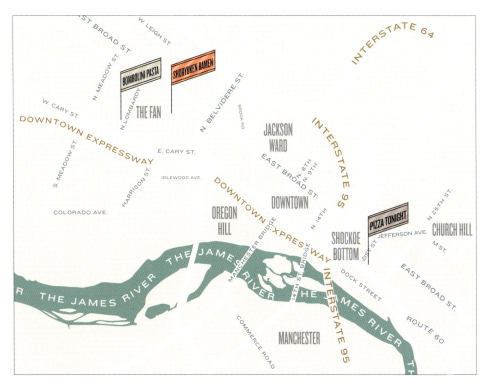

10
BOMBOLINI PASTA

JOHN KRECKMAN

Fresh Fettuccini

Fettuccini Carbonara

16
EARLY BIRD BISCUIT CO. & BAKERY

TIM LAXTON

Biscuits with Molasses Butter

22
PIZZA TONIGHT

VICTORIA DEROCHE

Fig and Pig Pizza

28
SHORYUKEN RAMEN

WILL RICHARDSON

Hiyashi Chuka

chef

JOHN KRECKMAN

recipes

FRESH FETTUCCINI

FETTUCCINI CARBONARA

BOMBOLINI PASTA

John Kreckman sees pasta as a blank slate, ready for anything. Stuffed pastas have infinite possibilities for fillings. Different flavors and colors can infuse sheets of dough.

"You can make whatever you want," he says. "The limit is your time and money."

That experimentation drives Bombolini Pasta where, John says, they're "always, always looking" for new flavors. He takes suggestions from customers and constantly refines and tweaks traditional standbys. He'll try anything twice before deciding it doesn't work, but plenty of winners arise from his search.

Some standouts? A cinnamon noodle, requested by family, that "was kind of odd, but it had a really good flavor to it." He also mixes dark chocolate powder in with the dry ingredients to create a South American mole-style noodle. "I had some people that did it as dessert," he says. "Some people did it with roast meats, so you've got that smoky chocolate base."

While the added flavors are seemingly limitless, the core ingredients for fresh pasta are simple. It's often the environment that can make the process tricky. Humidity or dryness in the air, outside temperatures that are too hot or cold, and the balance of gluten and protein in the flour can all change the final product.

"You make a lot of mistakes," he says. "There's no way around it. There are some things that are really easy to do and you can make the recipe exactly the same every time. There's no question to it. With pasta, it's always changing."

John says to just stick with it and eventually you'll learn what feels right.

"When you first make it, it looks horrible. It looks completely wrong," he says. "You roll it out, it looks bad, you fold it over and send it back through. The process of lamination stretches the dough out and it makes what looks like cottage cheese into a beautiful dough."

"Once you do it once or twice, you'll get it right. If you get it right the first time you need to go buy a lottery ticket or something."

And while he's all about pushing the limits, his approach also encourages simplicity—good food made with accessible ingredients prepared in inventive but uncomplicated ways.

"I don't want to cook labor-intensive dishes," he says. "I want you to sit with friends and shovel pasta in your mouth. It's not a pretty meal. It's designed to be good."

— BOMBOLINI PASTA —

"I DON'T WANT TO COOK LABOR-INTENSIVE DISHES. I WANT YOU TO SIT WITH FRIENDS AND SHOVEL PASTA IN YOUR MOUTH. IT'S NOT A PRETTY MEAL. IT'S DESIGNED TO BE GOOD."

—JOHN KRECKMAN

WHAT ARE YOUR GO-TO INGREDIENTS?

Mustard and cream. Everybody loves cream. It's not that healthy but it tastes good.

WHAT'S THE STRANGEST INGREDIENT YOU'VE EVER WORKED WITH?

I've got a container of sumac that I've been messing around with. It's citrusy and it's spicy and it's different.

WHAT WAS YOUR INTRODUCTION TO COOKING?

I worked for a lady a long time ago who owned the Stuart Circle Pharmacy, which is now Kuba Kuba. It was just a neighborhood pharmacy with 15 seats, a little deli counter, and the classic soda bar. She taught me a lot of stuff.

WHERE DO YOU GO OUT TO EAT?

I eat noodles when I go out and Pho So 1 is the go-to. I don't even really need the noodles. The broth is what I want.

WHAT'S YOUR FAVORITE DISH TO COOK FOR FAMILY AND FRIENDS?

My wife likes crepes and we'll do potato pancakes. I fry it up with meat inside or just straight up with a little dollop of sour cream and some salt and pepper. It's not fancy, but it's good.

WHAT'S YOUR FAVORITE KITCHEN MUSIC?

If we're closed, it's always really loud, energetic music—new pop music or house techno or something like that. It's as loud as it will go and we can yell and scream and just be loud and nobody cares.

WHAT'S THE LAST MEAL YOU MADE FOR YOURSELF?

The last meal I made was ham croquettes with a little bit of spicy sauce to go on a picnic. That's not what we usually have. Usually it's something stupid and lame, but you caught me on a good day.

— BOMBOLINI PASTA —

FRESH FETTUCCINI

YIELD: 2 SERVINGS

A recipe for fresh pasta is a suggested starting point. Protein and gluten counts in the flour, environmental factors—all can change the texture. If it's humid, try starting with less water; if it's dry, add a little more.

INGREDIENTS

1 C
ALL-PURPOSE
FLOUR

1 EGG

INSTRUCTIONS

1. Add flour to a large bowl and create a well in the center.
2. Break egg into well.
3. Beat egg with fork, incorporating flour as you go.
4. When egg and flour have come together, knead into a ball and flatten with a floured rolling pin.
5. Feed dough through a pasta machine on the thickest setting.
6. Reduce thickness gradually, passing dough through each setting until pasta is the desired thickness.
7. Dust pasta sheet with flour and cut into ¼-inch-wide noodles.

— BOMBOLINI PASTA —

FETTUCCINI CARBONARA

YIELD: 2 SERVINGS

INGREDIENTS

1 TBSP OLIVE OIL

2 STRIPS THICK BACON, CUT INTO SMALL STRIPS

⅓ C SMALL SWEET ONION, SLICED

¼ C FRESH PEAS

½ TBSP GARLIC, CHOPPED

½ C HEAVY CREAM

SALT AND PEPPER, TO TASTE

1 BATCH FRESH FETTUCCINI PASTA (RECIPE PG. 13)

INSTRUCTIONS

1. Add oil, bacon, onion, and peas to a large sauté pan over medium-high heat. Cook until bacon is crisp and onions have softened, about 8 minutes.

2. Add garlic and cook for additional 1 minute, being careful not to burn.

3. Add heavy cream and cook until thickened, 2–4 minutes. If it gets too thick, add a splash more cream to thin it.

4. Season with salt and pepper to taste.

5. Bring a large pot of salted water to a boil. Add fresh pasta and boil for 1–2 minutes. Taste pasta to test doneness.

6. Drain pasta and add to sauté pan with sauce and cook for 1 minute over medium-high heat. Serve immediately.

— BOMBOLINI PASTA —

EARLY BIRD BISCUIT CO. AND BAKERY

Elderly women walk into Early Bird Biscuit Co. and are transported back to younger days. Burly mechanics with grease under their nails step inside and get choked up. In fact, a lot of people—this writer included—get a little misty-eyed at the sight of a flour-covered rolling pin and the smell of baking biscuits.

"Biscuits kind of get people talking about their relatives making them and what they were like," says Early Bird owner Tim Laxton. "It's strikes an emotional chord with a lot of people."

Their stories aren't unlike Tim's. He remembers his grandfather teaching him to make the gravy he serves at Early Bird. His grandfather added a little flour to a pan of bacon fat and explained how to cook it off. "What I didn't know," Tim says, "is the guy was teaching me to make a roux. It's just the most basic, casual type of way to teach somebody how to do something."

But the roots of Early Bird truly rest with his maternal grandmother, Mattie Belle. The lady, he says, was known for her biscuits. "Every time that we would come together as a family, and we would have a sit-down meal, biscuits would be a part of that."

Tim carried on the tradition, making biscuits for parties, funerals, weddings, and holidays. Eventually he started toying with the idea of leaving his pool and spa company behind and opening a bakery. He happened upon a small space in Lakeside, tucked between a TV repair business and a magic and novelty shop.

From there, everything seemed to fall into place, albeit with a lot of work. In those early months, Tim would arrive at 4 o'clock in the morning and work 14 hours straight as baker, cashier, dishwasher, accountant, and inventory manager. "Looking back, I don't know how I did it," he says. "There were forces beyond any of this that were guiding me."

In addition to his grandmother's traditional buttermilk biscuits, Tim serves up a daily special, alternating between sweet combinations like strawberries and cream, and savory flavors like Parmesan black pepper. He turns out upwards of 450 biscuits every morning—all made nine or 10 at a time.

"When you're making biscuits, it's a gentle touch," he says. "Once you pull the ingredients together, just put it in the oven and let it be. My grandmother showed us to take care, that it's almost like watercolor painting. The more perfect you try to make it, the more imperfect it becomes."

CHEF

TIM
LAXTON

BISCUITS
WITH MOLASSES
BUTTER

— EARLY BIRD BISCUIT CO. & BAKERY —

WHAT ARE YOUR GO-TO INGREDIENTS?

Lemon zest, molasses, butter, buttermilk, local ham and sausage, Virginia-milled flour.

Butter would be at the top of the list though. That's the thing that makes things very special. I use so much butter in this bakery that I had a neon sign made.

WHAT'S THE STRANGEST INGREDIENT YOU'VE EVER WORKED WITH?

I made a biscuit glaze out of the Hardywood Gingerbread Stout. It was really amazing. Beer and biscuits go great together.

WHAT'S YOUR FAVORITE DISH TO COOK FOR FAMILY AND FRIENDS?

I love making Moroccan food. I actually brought a tagine back from Marrakesh that I bought on the streets. It's huge and I'm pretty proud of it. I like to break that out. I still have some Ras el Hanout [spice blend] in my freezer that I brought back from Marrakesh.

WHAT'S YOUR FAVORITE KITCHEN MUSIC?

M. Ward, The Black Keys, Father John Misty, and old dub. Bluegrass happens a lot.

It's kind of cool to just throw some odd stuff out now and then for the customers because they really dig it. Music's important and the customers have fun with that part of it. That's the fun thing is picking what the day might sound like.

"A biscuit's great, but a biscuit with something is amazing. My father used to place a pat of butter on a saucer, pour molasses over it, and mash it up. I added that as a condiment as an homage to my father."

—TIM LAXTON

— EARLY BIRD BISCUIT CO. & BAKERY —

BISCUITS WITH MOLASSES BUTTER

YIELD: 4 LARGE BISCUITS

"This is not fine cuisine," says Tim Laxton about his biscuits. "It's good old Southern cooking." But it's still a craft that requires quality ingredients and a careful, gentle touch. Just pull the ingredients together, cut the biscuits, and pop them in the oven.

Ingredients

FOR BISCUITS:

- 2 C SELF-RISING FLOUR
- 4 TBSP UNSALTED BUTTER, VERY COLD
- ¾ C WHOLE FAT BUTTERMILK
- 2 TBSP SALTED BUTTER, MELTED

FOR MOLASSES BUTTER:

- 3 TBSP SALTED BUTTER, ROOM TEMPERATURE
- 3 TSP MOLASSES

CONTINUES ON NEXT PAGE

— EARLY BIRD BISCUIT CO. & BAKERY —

IN THE KITCHEN WITH TIM LAXTON | BISCUITS WITH MOLASSES BUTTER

INSTRUCTIONS

FOR THE BISCUITS

1. Preheat oven to 450 degrees.

2. Add flour to a large mixing bowl.

3. Dip unsalted butter in flour to coat. This keeps the butter from sticking to the box grater. Grate butter into the bowl with the flour, patting the grater to fully empty butter shreds. This grating method creates air pockets inside the dough, adding an airy texture to the biscuits.

4. With your hands, toss butter and flour together gently. Be careful not to overwork the dough. The butter should stay as cold as possible.

5. Pour buttermilk directly into the mixture. Rotating the bowl, pull in the sides of the mixture with a spatula and gently fold butter, flour, and buttermilk together.

6. Once formed into a cohesive mound, gently knead the mixture on a floured surface until the dough forms a ball, about 1 minute. Be careful not to overwork the dough.

7. Gently flatten the dough using your hands.

8. Using a floured rolling pin, roll out the dough until it is uniformly 1 inch thick.

9. Coat the blade of a sharp knife with flour to prevent sticking. Cut the dough into 3-inch squares, trimming away rough edges.

10. Place biscuits onto an ungreased baking sheet and bake on the middle rack for 15–20 minutes, but checking after 10 minutes. When biscuits are golden brown, remove tray from the oven.

11. Brush each biscuit with melted salted butter. Allow biscuits to cool slightly before serving.

FOR THE MOLASSES BUTTER

» Place butter in a small shallow dish and drizzle with molasses. Using the back of a fork, mash the butter and molasses together and serve with warm biscuits.

— EARLY BIRD BISCUIT CO. & BAKERY —

IN THE KITCHEN WITH TIM LAXTON | BISCUITS WITH MOLASSES BUTTER

CHEF

VICTORIA DEROCHE

RECIPE

FIG AND PIG PIZZA

PIZZA TONIGHT

Not many chefs can say their business began in their backyard, but that's the story behind Pizza Tonight.

It began when Victoria DeRoche and her husband Joe purchased an outdoor oven to try their hand at wood-fired cooking.

"We watched three YouTube videos and thought we had mastered the art of wood-fired cooking," she says. "So after we cured the oven, I thought we would just pop it open and start cooking."

That first meal turned out to be a little more complicated. "The dogs wouldn't even eat it," she says. "We didn't talk to each other because it was just the worst."

Luckily, they stuck with it and eventually started hosting a monthly party, dubbed Pizza Club. Victoria would provide the dough and sauce and develop a signature cocktail. She gave attendees a prompt for toppings and first-timers had to make a pizza.

"Everyone would drink and eat tiny slivers of pizza, because we could only do one at a time," Victoria says.

While no one talks about Fight Club, the same couldn't be said for Pizza Club. Word spread among friends of friends and after two years, the crowd had grown too large.

So Victoria decided to equip people to have Pizza Club in their own homes. She created a pizza package with two doughs and a sauce that she could sell at farmers markets.

"The idea was great because it's so artisan," she says. "People can go to the farmers market and pick out fresh ingredients and make pizza… tonight."

From there, Victoria opened a mobile pizza oven for catering events and the occasional food truck roundup. Customers find typical cheese and pepperoni, but Victoria's cooking chops really shine on specialty pizzas like one of their top sellers, the fig and pig. The sweet and savory pizza is based on an appetizer of fresh figs stuffed with Gorgonzola and wrapped in prosciutto.

Or take the Cinco de Mayo pie-o—a red sauce base with chorizo, cilantro, Mexican crema, fresh avocado, and cheddar.

"Pizza's a vehicle for any flavors you want to present," she says. "There are purists and people that only want to do certain things, but you can have fun. It's just bread that you can make into anything."

Victoria may experiment with the pizza ingredients, but she's meticulous when it comes to using the wood-fired oven.

"It's not like sticking a pizza in your convection oven and just leaving it for 25, 30 minutes," she says. "You see the fire and you have to be attentive, you have to be intuitive."

— PIZZA TONIGHT —

WHAT ARE YOUR GO-TO INGREDIENTS?

Olive oil, garlic, salt, lemon. You can do anything with those.

WHERE DO YOU GO OUT TO EAT?

I love eating Asian food because it's so contrary to the flavor profiles of Italian. So things that are beyond my knowledge—ramen is fascinating to me, Korean barbecue is delicious. Anything that is opposite of what I can create.

WHAT'S YOUR FAVORITE DISH TO COOK FOR FAMILY AND FRIENDS?

I'm a go-to pasta girl. If people stop by and I'm making something from nothing, it's pasta. My favorite super-ghetto dish is aglio olio peperoncino, which is olive oil and garlic, and you just sauté that in a pan. You add hot peppers. You do your spaghetti. And when it comes out, you add toasted breadcrumbs.

WHAT'S YOUR FAVORITE KITCHEN MUSIC?

I don't know if I can pick any one thing. I have distinct memories of having dinner parties and that's the time when the Beastie Boys album dropped, or a Radiohead song came out when I was cooking that.

WHAT WAS YOUR INTRODUCTION TO COOKING?

My parents. My dad is the world's best chef. He can just stick his nose in the refrigerator for 10 minutes and come out with something that's just absolutely amazing. You become angry because it's so good.

WHAT'S THE LAST MEAL YOU MADE FOR YOURSELF?

Last night I made a family meal. My kids came over. It was black rice cooked with coconut milk, roasted kale with coconut flakes, topped with grilled salmon and a Sriracha-type sauce.

— PIZZA TONIGHT —

FIG AND PIG PIZZA

YIELD: 1–2 SERVINGS

This pizza is based on an appetizer—sliced fresh figs stuffed with Gorgonzola cheese, wrapped with prosciutto, and broiled. The savory and sweet pie has been a winner since it hit the menu, falling just behind the standard cheese and pepperoni pizzas.

INGREDIENTS

- 8 OZ PIZZA DOUGH
- 2 TBSP OLIVE OIL
- 3 TBSP FIG PRESERVES, ROOM TEMPERATURE
- 2–3 SLICES THIN PROSCIUTTO
- ¼ C GORGONZOLA OR BLUE CHEESE

PIZZA TONIGHT

IN THE KITCHEN WITH VICTORIA DEROCHE | FIG AND PIG PIZZA

INSTRUCTIONS

1. Preheat oven to 500 degrees.

2. Stretch pizza dough until it's 10–12 inches in diameter. Place dough onto a parchment-lined sheet pan or baking stone.

3. Drizzle olive oil over stretched dough. The oil will make spreading the fig preserves easier.

4. With the back of a spoon, spread fig preserves over the dough in a thin, even layer. The preserves act as a sauce.

5. Evenly place prosciutto over pizza.

6. Sprinkle with Gorgonzola or blue cheese.

7. Bake for 10–12 minutes or until crust is golden and preserves are bubbly and hot.

SHORYUKEN RAMEN

Shoryuken Ramen started as a simple solution to a simple problem. Will Richardson was tired of driving to D.C. and New York for "a potentially mediocre bowl of noodles." He wanted ramen readily available, all the time.

He started cooking up bowls of noodles in friends' kitchens. Then John Maher, owner of The Rogue Gentlemen, suggested a pop-up shop in his restaurant, which led to other pop-up dinners wherever Will could find a space. Then he approached Rick Lyons, owner of Lunch. and Supper!, about taking over Lunch. on Monday and Tuesday nights when the restaurant is dark.

By the second week, Lunch. was slammed and Shoryuken was selling out within minutes.

"The reception was so incredible," Will says. "It didn't take long before the whole thing was really bigger and moving faster than I could. It took on a life of its own and I'm the only one that could drive it I guess."

In fact, the hunger for ramen has been so strong that Shoryuken was able to open up a brick and mortar near Virginia Commonwealth University.

"Here in Richmond, no one has really started a restaurant this way before," he says. "One advantage we had with the pop-ups is that we were able to feel out our market. We tested the market in every possible way and we were able to really refine our recipes in a way that other places were not able to do."

The menu features dishes like Hiyashi Chuka, which Will says, "literally translates to cold Chinese." The dish is a cold, vinaigrette-dressed noodle with a mix of toppings like pickled radish, pickled shiitake mushrooms, and seasoned bamboo shoots. In the brick and mortar, Will has been able to expand the menu with small plates, rice bowls, and kushiyaki, "which is basically stuff on sticks, grilled."

"We knew coming out of the gate that it was a chancy thing for us, because people just know us for noodles," Will says. "But I also think it was time for us to prove that we do come from a different background and we can do other things."

Shoryuken sounds like a Cinderella story, but it's hardly a fairy tale. Will says their success really came down to a lot of hard work from a lot of people invested in the concept.

"I'm lucky to have this team that's followed me around from the very beginning," he says. "I couldn't even pay them until this past December. Having guys that would follow you for six months working for noodles and beer is a really lucky thing."

WILL RICHARDSON

HIYASHI CHUKA

— SHORYUKEN RAMEN —

WHAT ARE YOUR GO-TO INGREDIENTS?

Soy sauce. Oh my gosh, so much soy sauce. And saki. That's become my go-to alcohol for cooking.

WHAT'S YOUR FAVORITE DISH TO COOK FOR FAMILY AND FRIENDS?

When it comes to cooking for my grandparents, I try to stay away from a lot of the things that my grandma does better, because she's relentless. I know she loves me very much, but I could never make a wonton in front of her because it's either too tight, too big, not tight enough, or not big enough.

WHAT'S THE LAST MEAL YOU MADE FOR YOURSELF?

I can't recall. It's funny, people don't really know that chefs eat probably worse than most people. Our diets are terrible.

WHAT'S YOUR FAVORITE KITCHEN MUSIC?

'80s, Motown, classic rock.

WHAT'S THE STRANGEST INGREDIENT YOU'VE EVER WORKED WITH?

Fermented meats. That's a big one in the Asian world. I've been presented with some fermented meats before. It was a really cool idea and a person who was actually making them brought them to me. It's a really unique thing, but even I don't feel like we're ready for things like that.

WHERE DO YOU GO OUT TO EAT?

Metzger, The Rogue Gentlemen, Comfort, Brux'l.

WHAT WAS YOUR INTRODUCTION TO COOKING?

I was born and raised in a restaurant. Basically against my family's wishes, I set out after high school and I learned in some really nice French kitchens. I think that really gave me an advantage, because merging with the Asian techniques that I grew up with, it gave me more than one or two ways to do things.

> "I'M LUCKY TO HAVE THIS TEAM THAT'S FOLLOWED ME AROUND FROM THE VERY BEGINNING... HAVING GUYS THAT WOULD FOLLOW YOU FOR SIX MONTHS WORKING FOR NOODLES AND BEER IS A REALLY LUCKY THING."
>
> — WILL RICHARDSON

— SHORYUKEN RAMEN —

HIYASHI CHUKA

YIELD: 2 SERVINGS

While this version of *Hiyashi Chuka* is vegetarian-friendly, Will Richardson says the choices for cold toppings are really endless. Most of the ingredients can be found in Asian markets. Will recommends Tan A if you live in Richmond.

INGREDIENTS

- 2 5-OZ PACKS FRESH RAMEN NOODLES
- 6–8 TBSP HIYASHI DRESSING (RECIPE PG. 34)
- 1 TBSP SESAME OIL
- ½ C PICKLED DAIKON RADISH, JULIENNED (RECIPE PG. 34)
- ⅔ C MARINATED BAMBOO SHOOTS (RECIPE PG. 34)
- ⅔ C QUICK-PICKLED MUSHROOMS (RECIPE PG. 34)
- ⅓ C REHYDRATED WOOD EAR MUSHROOMS, JULIENNED
- ¼ C GREEN ONIONS, THINLY SLICED
- NORI GOMI FURIKAKE RICE SEASONING, TO TASTE
- TOGARASHI OR CAYENNE PEPPER, TO TASTE

— SHORYUKEN RAMEN —

IN THE KITCHEN WITH WILL RICHARDSON | HIYASHI CHUKA

INSTRUCTIONS

1. Cook noodles according to package instructions and chill immediately in an ice bath.

2. Put chilled noodles in a large mixing bowl with hiyashi dressing and sesame oil, mixing gently with tongs until noodles are well coated.

3. Portion dressed noodles into 2 bowls and top each with pickled daikon radish, marinated bamboo shoots, pickled mushrooms, wood ear mushrooms, and green onion. Add as much or as little of each topping as you like.

4. Sprinkle with nori gomi furikake and togarashi to taste.

— SHORYUKEN RAMEN —

HIYASHI DRESSING

- ¼ c sesame seeds
- 3 Tbsp miso
- ¼ tsp salt
- ¼ c water
- 3 Tbsp rice vinegar
- ½ tsp sambal chili paste
- ¼ c soy sauce
- 2 Tbsp sugar
- ½ tsp sesame oil

In a large mixing bowl, whisk all ingredients together thoroughly.

PICKLED DAIKON RADISH

- 1 c rice vinegar
- 1 c sugar
- 1 lb daikon radish
- 1 c water
- ¼ tsp turmeric
- ¼ c kosher salt

In a small saucepan over medium heat, add vinegar, water, sugar, and turmeric. Bring to a boil, stirring to dissolve sugar. Remove from heat and allow to cool.

Meanwhile, peel daikon radish and slice into ¼-inch thick rounds. If your daikon is very large, slice the rounds into semicircles. Place in a colander and sprinkle with salt. Mix well so daikon is evenly coated with salt. Place colander over a bowl and let drain for 1 hour.

Rinse salt off with a couple changes of water and dry well. Put rinsed daikon in a sterilized glass jar. Pour cooled brine through a coffee filter or cheesecloth-lined strainer into the jar and cover the radish slices. Refrigerate for at least 4 hours, preferably overnight. This will keep for about 2 weeks.

QUICK-PICKLED MUSHROOMS

- 2 c dried shiitake mushrooms
- ½ c soy sauce
- 2 c water
- ½ c rice vinegar
- ½ c sugar
- 1 oz piece fresh ginger, peeled

Pour hot water over mushrooms until covered. Rehydrate for up to 1 hour.

Cut off stems and slice into ¼-inch pieces.

Add rehydrated mushrooms to a medium saucepan and add all remaining ingredients.

Bring to a boil, then simmer for 30 minutes. Let mushrooms cool in liquid.

MARINATED BAMBOO SHOOTS

- 1 15-oz can bamboo shoots
- 1 c soy sauce
- 4 c water
- ¼ c sesame oil
- ⅓ c sugar

Rinse bamboo shoots and drain thoroughly.

Add bamboo shoots to a medium saucepan and add all remaining ingredients.

Bring to a boil, then simmer on low for 45 minutes, or until shoots are tender. Let bamboo shoots cool in liquid.

CHAPTER TWO
NEW AMERICAN

4 RESTAURANTS

13 RECIPES

Let's take an old recipe and make it new again. Let's put together clean and inventive plates that showcase local and organic food without being preachy. Let's expand our taco horizons into something that requires a fork. Yes, let's.

This chapter features four different takes on what we'd call New American cuisine. The chefs might not call it that—maybe because nobody is quite sure what "New American" is supposed to mean—but to us it means familiar favorites improved and maybe not quite as familiar. Simple things elevated and served with an unexpected twist.

But most importantly, these are the spots where you know what you want, you know how you want it, and you know it's going to be damn good.

— CHAPTER TWO: NEW AMERICAN —

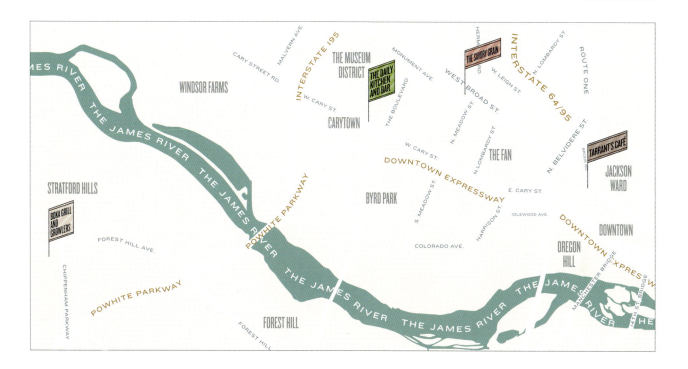

38
TARRANT'S CAFÉ

TED SANTARELLA

Rockfish Pan-Seared

She-Crab Soup

Coconut Raisin Bread Pudding with Whiskey Sauce

46
THE SAVORY GRAIN

SEAN MURPHY & JAMI BOHDAN

Shrimp and Grits

Crispy Stuffed Squash Blossoms

Rabbit Pot Pie

58
BOKA GRILL AND GROWLERS

PATRICK HARRIS

Pig and Fig Flautas

Crispy Skin Red Snapper

Café Mocha Crème Brûlée

68
THE DAILY KITCHEN AND BAR

MICHELLE WILLIAMS

Blackened Mahi Tacos

Wild Mushroom Bruschetta

Crispy Brussels Sprouts

Veggie Burger

TARRANT'S CAFÉ

MENU

ROCKFISH PAN-SEARED

SHE-CRAB SOUP

COCONUT RAISIN BREAD PUDDING WITH WHISKEY SAUCE

TED SANTARELLA

When talking to Ted Santarella, it seems like every item on the menu at Tarrant's Café is more than a list of ingredients. They all have a story.

The rockfish is his take on a pasta and chicken recipe from a past job in a Southside Italian restaurant. "It was a lunch special and I loved it," he says. "I worked for an old Italian man and he used to make fun of me because it was a nontraditional dish and I loved it so much."

Describing the bread pudding, he talks about Arlene Bjork, a yoga teacher who worked across the street and came in regularly. "We'd sit and she'd eat the whole bowl of bread pudding. It's meant for like five people," he says. "She passed away and I call it Arlene's bread pudding as a little homage to her."

These stories are emblematic of Ted's belief in enjoying the company of others over straightforward and honest

food in an environment that reminds people of home.

"The happy moments I remember as a child—the only time when nobody was arguing, when everyone dropped all the crap and just enjoyed each other's company—were around the kitchen table," he says. "Basically I'm just correcting my childhood and creating the same good feelings I had as a child around the kitchen table. That's how I earn my living."

That approach begins with a menu that tries to appeal to as many people as possible. It's hard to imagine now, but when Ted first opened Tarrant's Café, he cooked everything on the apartment stove upstairs and heated it up on a hot plate. Nearly a decade later, his brasserie-style restaurant has a seemingly endless menu ranging from simple soups and sandwiches to hearty steak dinners and seafood entrees like barramundi.

The warmth of Tarrant's extends to something a little more intangible. It's a staff of waiters and bartenders who are just plain nice. It's the exposed brick and tile floor, the chandeliers and tin ceilings—all an effort to recreate the old cafés of France and Italy.

It's the feeling of being in someone's home.

"Our nature is just to be sincere, honest, accommodating, nurturing," Ted says. "What we do is very intimate; people do this in their home."

"If friends come over to my house for dinner, it's not a potluck. You're coming to my house and I'm feeding you. I'm pulling out all of the stops for you. And that's how I run my business."

— TARRANT'S CAFÉ —

"...creating the same good feelings I had as a child around the kitchen table. That's how I earn my living."
—Ted Santarella

WHAT ARE YOUR GO-TO INGREDIENTS?

Seafood, extra virgin olive oil, garlic, fresh greens.

WHAT'S YOUR FAVORITE DISH TO COOK FOR FAMILY AND FRIENDS?

Thanksgiving dinner.

WHERE DO YOU GO OUT TO EAT?

I like to go to Can Can. The food is always original and creative. I love the atmosphere there. You can have a fancy meal with a $300 bottle of wine, or you can just go in and get a burger.

WHAT'S YOUR FAVORITE KITCHEN MUSIC?

Jazz, NPR news.

— TARRANT'S CAFÉ —

ROCKFISH PAN-SEARED

YIELD: 4 SERVINGS

This rockfish dish is loosely based on a chicken and pasta dish from Franco's, a former Southside restaurant where Ted Santarella once worked. At Tarrant's Café, this dish is served with seasonal vegetables and rice.

INGREDIENTS

- 4 8-OZ BONELESS, SKINLESS ROCKFISH FILETS
- SALT AND PEPPER, TO TASTE
- ½ C ALL-PURPOSE FLOUR
- 2 TBSP CLARIFIED BUTTER OR VEGETABLE OIL
- 2 TBSP BUTTER
- 6 LARGE GARLIC CLOVES, MINCED
- 1 TBSP CAPERS
- 1 C ARTICHOKE HEARTS, QUARTERED
- ½ C TOMATOES, DICED
- ¼ C PARSLEY, CHOPPED
- ¼ C PITTED KALAMATA OLIVES, SLICED IN HALF
- ½ C CHICKEN OR CLAM BROTH

INSTRUCTIONS

1. Preheat oven to 425 degrees.
2. Season both sides of rockfish filets with salt and pepper.
3. Put flour in a shallow dish or plate. Dredge fish in flour, shaking off any excess.
4. Heat clarified butter in a large sauté pan over medium-high heat. Add fish and sear 1–2 minutes per side, making sure to get a nice brown color. At this point, the fish is not completely cooked; it will be finished in the oven. Remove the fish from the pan and drain excess clarified butter.
5. Add fresh butter to the pan and melt over medium heat. Add garlic and cook for 30 seconds. Add all remaining ingredients and cook for 1 minute.
6. If skillet is not ovenproof, transfer vegetables to a baking dish. Nestle fish into vegetable mixture and cook in the oven for 7–14 minutes, or until the fish reaches 145 degrees.

— TARRANT'S CAFÉ —

SHE-CRAB SOUP

YIELD: 6–8 SERVINGS

Ted worked in Virginia Beach in the 1980s and saw how people would line up around the block for she-crab soup. "They were selling gallons and gallons of it," he says.

When he opened Tarrant's, he remembered that reaction and the soup became a must-have on the menu.

INGREDIENTS

- 5 TBSP BUTTER
- ¾ C ONIONS, CHOPPED
- ¾ C CELERY, CHOPPED
- 1 BAY LEAF
- 4 TBSP ALL-PURPOSE FLOUR
- 4 C WATER
- 2 TBSP CRAB BASE
- 2 TBSP PARSLEY, CHOPPED
- 1½ TSP DRIED THYME
- 1½ TSP BLACK PEPPER
- 8 OZ CLAW CRABMEAT
- 8 OZ SPECIAL CRABMEAT
- 2 C HALF-AND-HALF
- 1 C HEAVY CREAM
- ½ C CREAM SHERRY

INSTRUCTIONS

1. In a large pot, melt butter over medium heat. Add onions, celery, and bay leaf. Cook until vegetables are translucent, about 5 minutes.
2. Sprinkle flour over the vegetables and cook for an additional 1–2 minutes
3. Add water, crab base, parsley, thyme, black pepper, and crabmeat to the pot. Bring to a boil, then reduce to a simmer. Simmer until soup thickens, 8–10 minutes.
4. Add half-and-half, heavy cream, and sherry, and bring to just barely a simmer. Remove from heat and serve.

— TARRANT'S CAFÉ —

— TARRANT'S CAFÉ —

COCONUT RAISIN BREAD PUDDING WITH WHISKEY SAUCE

YIELD: 8-10 SERVINGS

Bread pudding is a simple dish with humble origins; it began as a way to use stale bread. Throw in some coconut, golden raisins, and whiskey sauce, and this unpretentious dessert turns into something worth raving about.

INGREDIENTS

FOR BREAD PUDDING:

- 1 TSP BUTTER, OIL, OR COOKING SPRAY TO GREASE PAN
- 8–10 C HEARTY WHITE BREAD, CUBED AND LEFT UNCOVERED OVERNIGHT
- 5 EGGS
- 2½ C HALF-AND-HALF
- 1 C SUGAR
- 2 TBSP VANILLA EXTRACT
- 1 STICK BUTTER, MELTED
- 1 TBSP CINNAMON
- 2 C SWEETENED SHREDDED COCONUT
- 1 C GOLDEN RAISINS

FOR SAUCE:

- 1½ TSP CORNSTARCH
- 1½ TSP WATER
- 2 C HEAVY CREAM
- 1 C LIGHT BROWN SUGAR
- 4 OZ WHISKEY
- 2 STICKS BUTTER

INSTRUCTIONS

1. Preheat oven to 350 degrees.
2. Grease a 13x9x2-inch baking dish and evenly spread bread into the dish.
3. In a large bowl, beat together eggs, half-and-half, sugar, vanilla extract, melted butter, and cinnamon. Mix in coconut.
4. Pour liquid mixture over the bread.
5. Sprinkle raisins on top, gently patting them down.
6. Cover with aluminum foil and bake 45–60 minutes, until liquid is completely absorbed.
7. Make sauce: In a very small bowl, mix cornstarch with water and set aside. Place all remaining ingredients in a medium saucepan and bring to a boil. Reduce to a simmer, stirring continuously. Add cornstarch slurry and simmer until thickened, 2–3 minutes.
8. Remove sauce from heat and serve over warm bread pudding.

— TARRANT'S CAFÉ —

THE SAVORY GRAIN

Jami Bohdan wasn't in the market to buy a restaurant when she walked by The Empress and saw it was for sale. She called the owner to ask why she was closing. She told Jami she wasn't looking for just anyone to sell to—that she wanted someone who knows and loves the industry.

At the time, Jami was the general manager just two doors down at The Republic, but the restaurant was preparing to close. So she went home that night and talked to her husband. "I told him, I know what I'm doing and I love this industry," she says. "It feels like a day later I bought a restaurant. It wasn't planned out, but it worked out nicely."

Jami spent four months renovating the space. She wanted to create an inviting atmosphere, much like the rustic charm of small pub she fell in love with in Vermont. The space already featured reclaimed wood and exposed brick, and a few church pews were left behind. Her husband and father-in-law handled most of the renovations and even built a family table from heart pine from an old Petersburg tobacco warehouse.

She also brought Sean Murphy on as executive chef. The two shared many of the same personal and professional orbits, but had never crossed paths. A mutual friend—from non-overlapping stints as manager and chef at Metro Bar and Grill in the Fan—suggested they meet and they turned out to be a perfect fit.

Jami and Sean worked together to develop a menu of seasonal, farm-to-table dishes like stuffed squash blossoms and rabbit pot pie. "We really collaborate well," Jami says. "Sean brings the majority of things to the table, but I've been able to say, 'I saw this,' or, 'can we try this and put our own spin on it?' There are a lot of signature dishes that we have now that people love. People come from near and far to get his shrimp and grits."

They also share a love of interacting with their customers and creating a backdrop to moments in their lives.

"It might sound a little cheesy, but I always feel

recipes

SHRIMP AND GRITS

CRISPY STUFFED SQUASH BLOSSOMS

RABBIT POT PIE

chef

Sean Murphy

owner

JAMI BOHDAN

like I'm trying to do a lot more than just fill somebody's belly," Sean says. "I'm making a memorable moment, a memorable experience. We have a lot of people that we've done engagement dinners for and then they come back and see us on their anniversary."

It's just the kind of experience Jami pictured, even as she was tearing down walls and painting chairs to build The Savory Grain.

"When we were renovating this place and my friends were here until the very last minute painting," she says, "I told them all, we're creating our family hangout for the rest of our lives."

— THE SAVORY GRAIN —

"I always feel like I'm trying to do a lot more than just fill somebody's belly. I'm making a memorable moment, a memorable experience."

—Sean Murphy

"When we were renovating this place and my friends were here until the very last minute painting, I told them all, we're creating our family hangout for the rest of our lives."

—Jami Bohdan

WHAT WAS YOUR INTRODUCTION TO COOKING?

Sean: I've always just enjoyed playing in the kitchen. The first recipe I made was a cheese waffle. I took a big waffle and toasted it and then melted cheese in the middle of it. We had a little breakfast bar in the house I grew up in, and I'd be serving cheese waffles over it when I was like six years old.

Jami: Making cookies and pies and cakes with my grandmothers.

WHAT ARE YOUR GO-TO INGREDIENTS?

Sean: It's hard not to say bacon. I've always got a little pork belly component, too, to make it a little more gourmet style.

Jami: Fresh veggies, hot sauce, cheese, local seafood.

WHAT'S THE STRANGEST INGREDIENT YOU'VE EVER WORKED WITH?

Sean: Rabbit mousse.

Jami: Beef heart or beef tongue.

WHERE DO YOU GO OUT TO EAT?

Sean: Mekong, Full Kee, Extra Billy's, my little local Mexican joint.

Jami: Stella's, Sidewalk Café, Lunch. and Supper!, Osaka, Azzurro.

WHAT'S THE LAST MEAL YOU MADE FOR YOURSELF?

Sean: The last thing I can remember making myself was a peanut butter and jelly sandwich in here on Monday. It's the last thing I can remember and I think it might be the last thing I made.

Jami: Seared tuna with Asian slaw and brown rice.

WHAT'S YOUR FAVORITE KITCHEN MUSIC?

Sean: '90s hip-hop and '80s.

Jami: The other day I put on Zeppelin radio and it's absolutely not allowed in the kitchen. I didn't know that.

― THE SAVORY GRAIN ―

SHRIMP AND GRITS
STONE-GROUND GOUDA GRITS WITH SHERRY CREAM SAUCE, BACON, AND TOMATO BRUSCHETTA

YIELD: 6 SERVINGS

Sean Murphy and Jami Bohdan bring a strong balance of creative chef and owner who knows what the customers want. A prime example? The Savory Grain's shrimp and grits. People come from near and far to get their fix.

INGREDIENTS

- 1 TBSP VEGETABLE OIL
- 6 SLICES THICK-CUT BACON, CHOPPED
- 2 LBS LARGE SHRIMP, PEELED AND DEVEINED
- 1 C SHERRY
- 1½ C HEAVY CREAM
- 1½ C BRUSCHETTA TOMATOES (RECIPE PG. 51)
- SALT AND PEPPER, TO TASTE
- 6 C COOKED GOUDA GRITS (RECIPE PG. 51)
- 3 TBSP BASIL, CHIFFONADE

INSTRUCTIONS

1. In a large sauté pan, heat vegetable oil over medium-high heat and add bacon. Cook until bacon just starts to crisp.
2. Add shrimp to pan and toss.
3. Carefully add sherry and flambé using a long match to ignite and cook off alcohol. (Note: Never add liquor from a bottle near an open flame.) Simmer until liquid has reduced by half.
4. Add heavy cream and simmer for about 1 minute.
5. Add bruschetta tomatoes, bring to a simmer, and cook until cream has reduced slightly, 3–4 minutes. Season with salt and pepper to taste.
6. Serve over stone-ground Gouda grits, spooning excess sauce around the plate, and garnish with basil.

— THE SAVORY GRAIN —

STONE-GROUND GOUDA GRITS

6 c water

¾ c heavy cream

4 Tbsp butter

2 Tbsp Worcestershire

1 Tbsp Frank's Red Hot sauce

1 Tbsp honey

1 tsp apple cider vinegar

1½ tsp roasted garlic, pureed

1½ tsp Cajun seasoning

½ tsp dried parsley

½ tsp dried basil

½ tsp smoked paprika

¼ tsp cayenne pepper

1½ c Byrd Mill stone-ground yellow grits

1 cob yellow corn, shucked

1 c smoked Gouda, shredded

Salt and pepper, to taste

In a large saucepan, bring water, heavy cream, and butter to a boil.

Stir in Worcestershire, hot sauce, honey, and apple cider vinegar. Then add roasted garlic puree, Cajun seasoning, parsley, basil, smoked paprika, and cayenne. Bring to a simmer.

Add grits and stir well. Bring to a simmer and cook for 25–35 minutes.

Note: If grits become too thick before they are done, add about ¼–½ cup water.

Add shucked corn and simmer for an additional 5 minutes.

Remove from the heat and stir in smoked Gouda until melted. Season with salt and pepper to taste. Cover with a lid and keep warm.

BRUSCHETTA TOMATOES

2 Tbsp olive oil

1½ Tbsp balsamic vinegar

1 tsp roasted garlic, pureed

1 tsp sugar

½ tsp salt

½ tsp pepper

3 medium tomatoes, seeded and chopped

2 Tbsp basil, chiffonade

Whisk together olive oil, balsamic vinegar, roasted garlic puree, sugar, salt, and pepper.

Pour dressing over chopped tomatoes.

Stir in basil and mix well. Taste and adjust salt and pepper if necessary.

— THE SAVORY GRAIN —

CRISPY STUFFED SQUASH BLOSSOMS

YIELD: 4 SERVINGS

Squash blossoms are one of summer's most delicate and delicious offerings. Buy as many as you can while they're in season and give this recipe a try. Sean stuffs his squash blossoms with goat cheese, crab, and peas—ingredients that complement the blossom's delicate flavor.

INGREDIENTS

- ¾ C GOAT CHEESE, SOFTENED
- ½ C COOKED PEAS, MASHED
- 1 EGG YOLK
- ZEST AND JUICE OF 1 LEMON, SEPARATED
- 4–5 SPRIGS THYME, LEAVES ROUGHLY CHOPPED
- SALT AND PEPPER, TO TASTE
- ½ C LUMP CRABMEAT (CHECK FOR SHELLS)
- 8 SQUASH BLOSSOMS
- 1 C ALL-PURPOSE FLOUR + 1 TSP FOR DUSTING
- ½ C CORNSTARCH
- ¼ C PILSNER OR LIGHTER STYLE BEER (CAN SUBSTITUTE WATER)
- 1 C VEGETABLE OIL, OR ENOUGH TO FILL PAN TO 1 INCH
- ½ C MINT PEA CRÈME FRAÎCHE (RECIPE PG. 53)
- 4 SPRIGS OF MINT
- ½ C BABY GREENS
- 8 PICKLED PERUVIAN RED PEPPERS

INSTRUCTIONS

Prepare crab filling

1. In a medium bowl, mix together goat cheese, mashed peas, egg yolk, zest and juice of ½ a lemon, and thyme. Add salt and pepper to taste.
2. Gently fold in crabmeat. Some lumps will break up as you mix, which is okay and even desirable. You want smaller pieces of crab throughout the filling, while maintaining as many larger pieces of meat as possible.
3. Transfer crab mixture into a piping bag fitted with a large plain tip. You want the opening to be large enough for crab to pass through.

Fill squash blossoms

1. Gently insert the corner of the piping bag all the way to the bottom of the blossom and pipe 1–2 tablespoons of filling. The blossom should be about ¾ filled. Lightly drape ends of petals in a crisscross pattern, covering the opening completely and sealing filling into the blossom.
2. Refrigerate filled squash blossoms for at least 30 minutes. Transfer them to the freezer for 8–10 minutes before frying.

Prepare batter

1. Do not make batter until after you have filled squash blossoms and are ready to fry.
2. Combine 1 c flour, cornstarch, and zest of ½ a lemon in a large bowl.
3. Slowly whisk in beer and juice of ½ a lemon until the batter has a pancake-like consistency.

— THE SAVORY GRAIN —

Fry squash blossoms

1. Fill a large cast-iron skillet or frying pan with 1 inch of vegetable oil.

2. Heat oil over medium-high heat until it reaches 350 degrees. You can test by dropping a smidge of batter into the hot oil. It should sizzle immediately without burning.

3. Remove blossoms from freezer and dust lightly with reserved flour on all sides, shaking off excess.

4. Dip blossoms into batter, coating evenly and letting excess drip off.

5. Immediately place in hot oil. Fry for 45 seconds–1 minute on each side, until pale golden brown.

6. Drain on paper towels and allow to cool slightly before transferring to serving plates.

7. Finish each plate with 2 tablespoons mint pea crème fraîche, then top with 2 squash blossoms. Garnish each serving with ⅛ cup baby greens, a sprig of mint, and 2 pickled peppers.

MINT PEA CRÈME FRAÎCHE

½ c fresh peas, cooked and pureed	¼ c heavy cream	30 mint leaves, chiffonade
1 c sour cream	Zest and juice of ½ lemon	Salt and pepper, to taste

In a large bowl, mix together peas, sour cream, heavy cream, and lemon zest and juice.

Fold in mint and season with salt and pepper to taste.

— THE SAVORY GRAIN —

RABBIT POT PIE

YIELD: 10 SERVINGS

For those who have never cooked with rabbit, the prospect can seem intimidating. But once you try it, you'll realize it's no more difficult than preparing a whole chicken. This hearty pot pie recipe is a great introduction to rabbit. At The Savory Grain, this dish is served with a simple parsnip puree and sweet pea mash (recipes pg. 57).

INGREDIENTS

2 MEDIUM RABBITS

3 TBSP SALT

3 TBSP PEPPER

3 TBSP MIXED HERBS (THYME, PARSLEY, SAGE, ROSEMARY), CHOPPED

4 TBSP OLIVE OIL, CANOLA OIL, OR VEGETABLE OIL BLEND

4 TBSP + ½ LB (2 STICKS) BUTTER

1 HEAD CELERY

2 CARROTS, ROUGHLY CHOPPED + 2 C CARROTS, DICED AND BLANCHED

1 LARGE YELLOW ONION

4 QT WATER

64 OZ SPRING ALE, HEFEWEIZEN, OR BELGIAN ALE

4 BAY LEAVES

3 TBSP ROASTED GARLIC

JUICE OF 2 LEMONS

2 C FLOUR

2 C PEAS, BLANCHED

10 5-INCH SQUARES PUFF PASTRY

1 EGG, BEATEN

THYME, PARSLEY, AND SAGE

IN THE KITCHEN WITH SEAN MURPHY | RABBIT POT PIE

INSTRUCTIONS

PREPARE POT PIE FILLING

1. Lay rabbits on a clean cutting board. Remove the legs at the joint. Generously season each side of the rabbit with about 1½ tablespoons salt, 1½ tablespoons pepper, and 1½ tablespoons mixed herbs.

2. Heat 2 tablespoons oil in a large cast-iron skillet over high heat. (An olive and vegetable oil blend works best because you can reach a higher smoking temperature.) Once oil just begins to smoke, add 2 tablespoons of butter and immediately add rabbits to the pan with the backside down and the ribcage facing up. Sear each side for 3–4 minutes until golden brown.

3. Heat 2 tablespoons oil and 2 tablespoons butter in a large stockpot over high heat. Coarsely chop celery, 2 carrots, and onion into ½-inch chunks and add to pot. Cook for 3–4 minutes, or until vegetables have some color.

4. Add water, beer, bay leaves, roasted garlic, and lemon juice. Whisk everything together and add seared rabbits. Bring to a boil, then reduce to a medium simmer. Cover partially and simmer for about 45 minutes. You want the meat to be tender and falling off the bone, without completely deteriorating. Once rabbits are at this point, turn off the stockpot and carefully remove them. Allow them to cool and then pull all the meat off the bones. This is best done while the meat is still warm but cool enough to handle. Be careful to avoid any small bones. Set pulled meat aside.

THE SAVORY GRAIN

IN THE KITCHEN WITH SEAN MURPHY | RABBIT POT PIE

5. Strain braising liquid and set aside.

6. In a medium saucepan, melt ½ pound butter over medium heat. Add flour, stirring continuously for 6–7 minutes, or until the mixture just barely takes on a light brown color. This is your blond roux.

7. Return strained stock to stockpot and return to a boil, then reduce to a simmer. Add the roux, a tablespoon or two at a time, until it reaches a thick velvety consistency. Add remaining salt, pepper, and mixed herbs to taste. Reserve about 1 cup of gravy for garnish.

8. Add 2 cups diced and blanched carrots, peas, and pulled rabbit meat to gravy. Mix thoroughly and make sure all ingredients are hot throughout.

BAKE AND FILL PUFF PASTRY

1. Preheat oven to 350 degrees.

2. Using a sharp knife, cut puff pastry into 5-inch squares. Work quickly so the pastry will stay as cold as possible. Score a ½-inch border around all four sides of each square. Fold over edges along score marks, creating a raised border. This will allow the center to puff up.

3. Brush the dough with an egg wash and bake for 8–10 minutes. Allow pastry to cool.

4. Using a sharp paring knife, cut the top off the center "puff" so you can fill the pastry. Reserve top.

5. Fill center of pastry with the pot pie filling and drizzle the plate with the reserved gravy. Serve with pastry top propped against the pie.

PARSNIP PUREE

10 parsnips	¾ c heavy cream
7 Tbsp butter	Salt and pepper, to taste

Bring a large pot of salted water to a boil.

Peel parsnips and cut into ¼-inch cubes.

Boil parsnips until soft enough to mash, 10–15 minutes. Strain.

While warm, mash with butter and heavy cream. Season with salt and pepper to taste.

SWEET PEA MASH

2½ c fresh peas	2 Tbsp fresh lemon juice	Salt and pepper, to taste

Bring a large pot of salted water to a boil. Also prepare a bowl of ice water to shock peas when they come out of the water.

Boil peas until soft enough to mash, about 10 minutes. Strain and quickly place in the ice water. This helps retain a bright green color.

Strain chilled peas and puree with lemon juice. Add salt and pepper to taste.

BOKA GRILL AND GROWLERS

When Patrick Harris signed up for a home economics class in 7th grade, he didn't really know what to expect. But he ended up being a natural in the culinary arts. He stuck with it and even went on to place among the top 10 in a Johnson and Wales University competition for high school chefs with his rendition of honey-glazed turkey roulades with wild mushroom-walnut duxelle.

He considered culinary school, but instead opted to study marketing at George Mason University. He worked his way through some of the D.C. area's top restaurants to pay his way. After graduation he combined his business savvy and love of food to open his first business—a catering company.

Patrick eventually left D.C. behind to lead the kitchen opening at Carytown's Water Grill and soon found another opportunity to start out on his own, this time in the burgeoning food truck trend. It was all the rage in L.A., but hadn't quite made it to the East Coast. So Patrick found a truck online, took out a loan, and set up shop.

With Boka Tako Truck, Patrick pulled from his past restaurant experiences—ranging from classical French to Asian fusion to upscale American—to develop his own flavor fusion, all wrapped up in a "tako."

He had to create demand in a market where gourmet food trucks didn't exist and where tacos had never been so loosely defined. As other trucks appeared on the scene, Patrick rallied them together to open Richmond's first food truck court at the Virginia Historical Society.

"Because of the uniqueness of what we were doing and its impact on Richmond's dining scene, we ended up getting tons and tons of PR," he says. "There was a lot of excitement and momentum that was built around us, and we were constantly pushing the envelope."

As Patrick found more ways to grow the business, he was able to expand into a larger commissary kitchen, add more trucks, and eventually open two brick and mortar restaurants—Boka Grill and Growlers in Southside and Boka Tako Bar in the Fan.

Today, there's still the "crazy truck chef" that pushes creative limits with specials like the duck tongue and unagi eel "surf and turf" taco. But Patrick now has a place to showcase other dishes, like the crispy skin red snapper with piquillo bouillabaisse, smoked grape and shallot salad, and crispy potato.

"Boka Grill allows me a lot more of that culinary freedom," he says. "People know they can always get that go-to gauntlet sampler of tacos, but we use that as a platform to play upward on the rest of our menu."

CHEF

PATRICK HARRIS

RECIPES

PIG AND FIG FLAUTAS

CRISPY SKIN RED SNAPPER

CAFÉ MOCHA CRÈME BRÛLÉE

— BOKA GRILL AND GROWLERS —

WHAT ARE YOUR GO-TO INGREDIENTS?

Agave, rice wine vinegar, lime, salt.

WHERE DO YOU GO OUT TO EAT?

I like Foo Dog. It's just good, quick, hearty food.

WHAT'S YOUR FAVORITE DISH TO COOK FOR FAMILY AND FRIENDS?

Pan-seared fish with some sort of savory starch and aromatic broth, with a crispy garnish and a sweet acid element, like a relish or a compote or a good salsa. That model is my favorite.

WHAT'S YOUR FAVORITE KITCHEN MUSIC?

I like a quiet kitchen. I'm good with my thoughts. Every once in a while, music will be back there, but I prefer music to clean than music to cook. When I clean, it's typically fast, hard, or angry music. Anything I can break a sweat to and push faster.

WHAT'S THE STRANGEST INGREDIENT YOU'VE EVER WORKED WITH?

Duck tongues, because they have this little bone or cartilage piece inside and you have to flip the tongue inside out and pull off the meat. You end up with an inside-out duck tongue.

— BOKA GRILL AND GROWLERS —

PIG AND FIG FLAUTAS

YIELD: 4 SERVINGS

This seemingly simple dish is layered with complex flavors. For Patrick Harris, just one type of pork wouldn't suffice—this dish incorporates rich pork belly, smoked bacon, and local Surry sausage.

INGREDIENTS

- 12 OZ PORK BELLY
- 3 CLOVES
- PEEL OF ¼ ORANGE, PITH REMOVED
- 1 SPRIG THYME
- 1 SHALLOT, MINCED
- 1 CLOVE GARLIC, MINCED
- 4 OZ HICKORY SMOKED BACON
- 4 OZ GROUND SURRY SAUSAGE
- ½ TBSP VEGETABLE OIL
- ½ TBSP BUTTER
- ½ ONION, THINLY SLICED
- 1 TBSP APPLE CIDER VINEGAR
- ½ TBSP SHERRY VINEGAR
- 1 TSP MAPLE SYRUP
- ½ TSP BROWN SUGAR
- ½ TSP WHITE SUGAR
- ½ TSP LIME JUICE
- 12 8-INCH FLOUR TORTILLAS
- OIL FOR FRYING
- 2 TBSP MAYONNAISE
- 1 TSP SRIRACHA
- FIG-GINGER COMPOTE (RECIPE PG. 62)
- 2 TBSP KECAP MANIS (A SWEET INDONESIAN SOY SAUCE WITH THE CONSISTENCY OF SYRUP)
- SALT, TO TASTE

SPECIAL EQUIPMENT

- TOOTHPICKS

CONTINUES ON NEXT PAGE →

— BOKA GRILL AND GROWLERS —

INSTRUCTIONS

1. Preheat oven to 300 degrees.

2. Add pork belly to a casserole dish that will fit the pork snugly. Place cloves, orange peel, and thyme in a spice sachet and add to the dish. Add shallot and garlic and cover everything with water, making sure the pork belly is fully submerged. Wrap with aluminum foil and bake until meat is completely tender, about 3–3½ hours.

3. Remove pork belly from braising liquid and cool until it can be handled. Shred meat and fat into a bowl and pour about ¼ cup of the braising liquid over it. Set aside.

4. In a large skillet, cook bacon until most of the fat is rendered, then chop into small pieces. Set aside.

5. Sauté sausage until browned. Set aside.

6. Heat vegetable oil and butter in a sauté pan over medium heat. Add onion and cook until a deep, golden color, about 15 minutes. You can deglaze the pan with a splash of water to pull up and redistribute the sugars as they caramelize. This should yield about 2 tablespoons of caramelized onions. Season with salt to taste.

7. In a large bowl, toss together shredded pork belly, sausage, bacon, and caramelized onions. Mix in the vinegars, maple syrup, sugars, and lime juice. Add salt to taste.

8. Warm flour tortillas in a pan or in the microwave to soften. Spoon about 1½ tablespoons of the pork mixture into each tortilla and fold in the sides, tucking the edges as you roll. The flautas should look like mini burritos and be closed on all sides. Skewer flautas with a toothpick through the edge of the seam so it doesn't open up during frying.

9. Preheat a deep fryer or pot of oil to 375 degrees.

10. Fry flautas until golden brown. Drain on paper towels.

11. In a small bowl mix together mayonnaise and sriracha. Add a few drops of water to loosen so it's easy to drizzle.

12. To serve, streak a heaping tablespoon of fig-ginger compote on each of four serving plates. Top the compote with 3 flautas and drizzle with sriracha mayonnaise and kecap manis.

FIG-GINGER COMPOTE

¼ c dried figs	1 Tbsp ginger juice (liquid from grated ginger that has been squeezed)	2 Tbsp sugar
¼ c water		Salt, to taste
1 Tbsp lime juice		

Add all ingredients except sugar and salt to a saucepan and bring to a boil. Cook until figs are tender. Add sugar and mix until dissolved, then remove from heat.

Puree with an immersion blender or in a stand blender. Season with salt to taste.

— BOKA GRILL AND GROWLERS —

CRISPY SKIN RED SNAPPER WITH PIQUILLO BOUILLABAISSE, SMOKED GRAPE SALAD, AND POTATO CRISPS

YIELD: 6 SERVINGS

Bouillabaisse is a Provençal fish stew with rustic roots. At Boka, this classic dish is updated and deconstructed. The essence of snapper is concentrated into a rich sauce and topped with crispy snapper. Smoked grape salad and potato crisps add texture and sophistication.

INGREDIENTS

- 6 6-OZ RED SNAPPER FILETS, SCALED AND SKIN LEFT ON
- ½ TBSP SALT
- ¾ C RICE FLOUR
- 2 TBSP VEGETABLE OIL
- 2 TBSP + 2 TBSP BUTTER
- HERB VINAIGRETTE (RECIPE PG. 65)
- PIQUILLO BOUILLABAISSE (RECIPE PG. 65)
- 1 C LONG-GRAIN WHITE RICE, COOKED
- ½ C BLACK BEANS, DRAINED AND WARMED
- SMOKED GRAPE SALAD (RECIPE PG. 65)
- POTATO CRISPS (RECIPE PG. 65)
- 2 TBSP MICRO GREENS

INSTRUCTIONS

1. Season snapper filets on both sides with salt and dust with rice flour, shaking off any excess.

2. Add vegetable oil to a large nonstick skillet over high heat. Add the fish, skin-side down, to the pan. Place a steak weight or small skillet on the fish, and reduce heat to medium. Cook until skin is crisp and flesh is cooked to white ⅓ of the way up the edge of the filet, 2–3 minutes depending on the thickness.

3. Flip filet and add 2 tablespoons of butter to pan. Baste fish with melted butter and cook on medium heat for additional 4 minutes.

4. Add herb vinaigrette to pan and remove from heat. Let fish rest for 1–2 minutes. Just before serving, baste fish once more with pan sauce.

5. In a clean skillet, add bouillabaisse and bring it to a simmer. Remove from heat, add remaining 2 tablespoons of butter, and stir until melted and mixed through.

6. In a large bowl, mix together cooked rice and warmed beans.

7. To serve, place about 4 ounces of bouillabaisse in each serving bowl. Tightly pack about ¼ cup of rice and beans in a ring mold and place in the center of the bowl, pressing down. Gently unmold. Top rice with fish, skin side up. Place a heaping spoonful of grape salad on top, and garnish with a few potato crisps and a sprinkle of micro greens.

— BOKA GRILL AND GROWLERS —

— BOKA GRILL AND GROWLERS —

PIQUILLO BOUILLABAISSE

- 1 sprig thyme
- 1 bay leaf
- 6 peppercorns
- 4 oz red snapper trimmings (you can get this from a fish monger or from trimming your own snapper)
- 4 c water
- ¼ c white wine
- 3 roasted piquillo peppers
- ¼ c fennel, coarsely chopped
- 2 Tbsp onion, chopped
- 1 celery rib, chopped
- 1 clove garlic, crushed
- 1½ tsp tomato paste
- 1 Tbsp lemon juice
- Salt, to taste

Add thyme, bay leaf, and peppercorns to an herb sachet.

In a large pot, add the sachet and all ingredients, except lemon juice and salt, and bring to a boil. Reduce to a simmer and cook for about 45 minutes.

Remove herb sachet and puree soup with an immersion blender or in batches in a stand blender.

Add lemon juice and salt to taste.

Strain the soup through a chinois or fine mesh sieve without pressing the solids through the sieve.

HERB VINAIGRETTE

- 3 Tbsp canola oil
- 1½ Tbsp rice wine vinegar
- ¼ tsp shallot, minced
- ¼ tsp garlic, minced
- ¼ tsp basil, minced
- ¼ tsp oregano, minced
- ¼ tsp parsley, minced
- Pinch of red pepper flakes
- Salt, to taste

Whisk together all ingredients and add salt to taste.

POTATO CRISPS

- 1 small russet potato
- 2–3 c olive oil for frying
- Sea salt, to taste

Scrub potato clean, and slice on a mandolin to about 1/16-inch thick.

Rinse potato slices three times in cold water. Pat completely dry.

In a shallow pan, add olive oil up to 1 inch. Heat oil to 350 degrees.

Fry potato slices until golden brown, then remove them with a slotted spoon onto paper towels. Season with sea salt.

SMOKED GRAPE SALAD

- 1½ Tbsp lime juice
- 1 Tbsp champagne vinegar
- 1 Tbsp agave
- 2 Tbsp sugar
- 1 Tbsp fresh mint, chiffonade
- 1 Tbsp shallot, minced
- 1 tsp salt
- 1 c seedless red grapes, quartered

SPECIAL SUPPLIES

- 1 handful wood chips

In a small bowl, whisk together all ingredients except grapes.

Pour marinade over grapes and toss. Set aside.

Soak wood chips in water for 1 hour, then drain.

Place chips in a large metal container, then scorch the wood with a torch until it lights on fire. Burn down to embers until they begin to smolder.

Place the bowl of marinated grapes in a large pot and surround with smoldering chips. Cover the pot with a lid and let grapes capture the smoke for 1½–3 minutes. The grapes will be "kissed" with smoke. The longer you expose them, the stronger the smoke essence.

— BOKA GRILL AND GROWLERS —

— BOKA GRILL AND GROWLERS —

CAFÉ MOCHA CRÈME BRÛLÉE

YIELD: 8 SERVINGS

Crème brûlée is a perfect canvas for creative flavors. At Boka, Patrick turns a coffee shop favorite, the café mocha, into dessert.

INGREDIENTS

- 1 QT HEAVY CREAM
- 3 TBSP COFFEE, COARSELY GROUND
- 4 EGGS + 3 EGG YOLKS
- ¾ C + 8 TBSP WHITE SUGAR
- ¼ TSP SALT
- 2 TBSP BITTERSWEET CHOCOLATE, FINELY CHOPPED
- ½ C CARAMEL SAUCE

INSTRUCTIONS

1. In a saucepan, bring heavy cream to a simmer, then remove from heat. Stir in coffee grounds and let steep until cream has cooled. Strain out the coffee grounds and set aside.

2. Preheat oven to 275 degrees.

3. In a large bowl, beat together eggs and egg yolks, ¾ cup sugar, and salt. Mix in the finely chopped chocolate.

4. Return the strained heavy cream to a saucepan and add caramel sauce. Bring to a simmer while stirring continuously. Once caramel has fully dissolved, remove from heat.

5. While whisking, slowly add about ½ cup of the hot cream mixture to the bowl with the eggs. This tempers the eggs so they don't scramble. Still whisking, slowly pour in the remaining cream and mix until chocolate has fully melted and custard is smooth.

6. Strain the custard through a chinois or fine mesh sieve to remove any curdled eggs or chocolate that did not melt.

7. Distribute the custard mixture evenly into 5-ounce ramekin dishes.

8. Place the ramekins into a casserole or roasting pan and fill the pan with water until it is halfway up the ramekins, creating a water bath.

9. Bake for 1 hour and 45 minutes, or until custard is set and a toothpick inserted into it comes out clean.

10. Refrigerate until cool. To finish, coat chilled custard with a layer of sugar (about 1 tablespoon per ramekin), and torch the sugar to create a golden brown candy shell.

THE DAILY KITCHEN AND BAR

 MENU | **BLACKENED MAHI TACOS** | **WILD MUSHROOM BRUSCHETTA** | **CRISPY BRUSSELS SPROUTS** | **VEGGIE BURGER**

In today's constantly changing food scene, not many people could imagine opening a restaurant at 21 years old, much less forming a partnership of owners that would continue to open restaurants for two decades.

But that's just what Michelle Williams, Jared Golden, and Ted Wallof have done in Richmond. As the Richmond Restaurant Group's first endeavor, The Hard Shell, turns 20, their most recent, The Daily Kitchen and Bar, celebrates just two years in Carytown—and more are on the horizon.

"If you asked my 21-year-old self if I would have four, five, six, 10 restaurants," Michelle says, "I would have said, 'let's just get this one functioning properly and making money.'"

With each restaurant, Michelle and her partners set out to create a unique concept, from food and drink menus to atmosphere and space design. In opening The Daily, they wanted to mimic a concept they'd seen while traveling in other cities—health-conscious, environmentally friendly, and socially responsible food with an extensive selection of vegetarian, vegan, and gluten-free dishes.

Michelle had to stretch her culinary background in seafood-driven restaurants, which rely on liberal use of butter and cream. At The Daily, she developed a menu that had the same satisfying and fulfilling flavor profiles, while using almost no sugar, butter, or cream. "It's what makes me passionate about what I do," she says. "After 20 years, I'm still learning."

She found that coconut milk can take the place of cream, such as in their vegan tomato bisque. Pureed nuts or tapioca starch can take on the characteristics of cheese for a pizza topping and, Michelle says, you won't even miss the mozzarella. "For a year and a half, we were trying these recipes on vegans and non-vegans alike."

She also revisited vegetarian staples that she says can sometimes be an

 CHEF MICHELLE WILLIAMS

afterthought. Instead, she wanted to create dishes—like the veggie burger and Brussels sprouts—that even a carnivore would love.

In the end, though, a strong partnership is possibly the key ingredient to their menu, and their longevity.

"We have a team approach to everything we do," Michelle says. "Jared is interested in what will be great items to share and what is appropriate for the mainstream population. Ted practices a plant-based lifestyle, so he is very passionate about making sure that options are plentiful for vegans and vegetarians, and that those dishes aren't an afterthought. I try to incorporate those two principles while still being true to my roots as a chef and offer a good mix of options for all palates."

— THE DAILY KITCHEN AND BAR —

"WE HAVE A TEAM APPROACH TO EVERYTHING WE DO. JARED IS INTERESTED IN WHAT WILL BE GREAT ITEMS TO SHARE AND WHAT IS APPROPRIATE FOR THE MAINSTREAM POPULATION. TED PRACTICES A PLANT-BASED LIFESTYLE, SO HE IS VERY PASSIONATE ABOUT MAKING SURE THAT OPTIONS ARE PLENTIFUL FOR VEGANS AND VEGETARIANS, AND THAT THOSE DISHES AREN'T AN AFTERTHOUGHT. I TRY TO INCORPORATE THOSE TWO PRINCIPLES WHILE STILL BEING TRUE TO MY ROOTS AS A CHEF AND OFFER A GOOD MIX OF OPTIONS FOR ALL PALATES."

—MICHELLE WILLIAMS

WHAT ARE YOUR GO-TO INGREDIENTS?

At the restaurant: Brussels sprouts (we would have a revolt if we ever took those off the menu), avocados, kale, and high-quality meat and fish. At home: My house would crumble without lots of pickled things and tomatoes.

WHAT'S THE LAST MEAL YOU MADE FOR YOURSELF?

Vegetarian tacos with all the fixings. Everything from scratch, except the tortillas.

WHAT WAS YOUR INTRODUCTION TO COOKING?

I worked at Tobacco Company as a hostess and cocktail waitress in high school. I spent a lot of time asking questions in the kitchen. The chef convinced me to take classes to learn how to cook. I knew my first day at my first kitchen job that this was going to be my career.

WHERE DO YOU GO OUT TO EAT?

Mamma Zu, Heritage, Stella's.

WHAT'S THE STRANGEST INGREDIENT YOU'VE EVER WORKED WITH?

Kelp noodles are pretty unusual. We have been trying to craft a way to use them in a dish that would be suitable for gluten-free and Paleo diets.

WHAT'S YOUR FAVORITE DISH TO COOK FOR FAMILY AND FRIENDS?

We eat a lot of seafood, especially in the summer. We grow our own oysters, so they are plentiful. I create dishes at home based on what's in the fridge, or what was caught fishing that day. My brother would tell you that eating a family meal with my husband (who's also a chef) and me is like an episode of *Chopped*.

WHAT'S YOUR FAVORITE KITCHEN MUSIC?

I need something upbeat. I like old-school classic rock best. It takes me back to my first job and all of the amazing things I learned from the guys who helped make me who I am today.

— THE DAILY KITCHEN AND BAR —

BLACKENED MAHI TACOS
WITH PICKLED RED CABBAGE SLAW, PICO DE GALLO, AND CILANTRO-LIME EMULSION

YIELD: 8 TACOS

"If we ever took our fish tacos off the menu," says Michelle Williams, "we would be in trouble." That's because these tacos are more than fish and slaw on a basic tortilla. Michelle tried 50 tortillas until they found the right one. From there, she layers flavors like vinegar, corn, tomatoes, and cilantro to create "the ultimate dish."

INGREDIENTS

- ½ C BLACKENING SEASONING (RECIPE PG. 73)
- 1½ LB FRESH MAHI
- 2 TBSP VEGETABLE OIL
- 8 SMALL FLOUR OR 16 CORN TORTILLAS (CORN TORTILLAS ARE MORE FRAGILE SO USE 2 PER TACO)
- 6 TBSP CILANTRO-LIME EMULSION (RECIPE PG. 73)
- 8 TBSP PICO DE GALLO (RECIPE PG. 73)
- 1½ C PICKLED RED CABBAGE SLAW (RECIPE PG. 73)
- 2 RIPE AVOCADOS, CUT INTO SLICES
- 2 SMALL LIMES, CUT INTO WEDGES

INSTRUCTIONS

1. Put blackening seasoning on a plate and roll mahi in it to fully coat.
2. Heat vegetable oil in a large sauté pan over medium-high heat and cook mahi, 3–4 minutes per side. Set cooked fish on a cutting board and wipe pan thoroughly. Cut fish into pieces that will easily fit in a taco.
3. If available, grill tortillas for 15 seconds per side. Alternatively, use a hot pan to warm tortillas.
4. Fill each tortilla with about 2 teaspoons of cilantro-lime emulsion and equal parts mahi. Top with 1 tablespoon pico de gallo and about ⅛ cup red cabbage slaw. Add a slice of avocado and serve with a slice of lime on the side.

— THE DAILY KITCHEN AND BAR —

BLACKENING SEASONING

- 1 Tbsp sweet paprika
- 2½ tsp salt
- 1 tsp onion powder
- 1 tsp garlic powder
- 1 tsp cayenne pepper
- ¾ tsp white pepper
- ¾ tsp black pepper
- ½ tsp dried thyme leaves
- ½ tsp dried oregano leaves

Mix all ingredients together.

PICO DE GALLO

- 4 large tomatoes, small dice
- 1 red onion, small dice
- 1 jalapeño pepper, small dice
- 1 bunch cilantro, finely chopped
- 3 limes, zest and juice
- ¼ c fresh corn, blanched
- Salt and pepper, to taste

Combine all ingredients in a large bowl and mix thoroughly. Season with salt and pepper to taste.

PICKLED RED CABBAGE SLAW

- 2 c rice wine vinegar
- 2 c apple cider vinegar
- 2 c water
- 2 c granulated sugar
- 2 Tbsp salt
- 1 large red cabbage, cored and very thinly sliced
- 2 red onions, thinly sliced
- 1 c cilantro, chopped
- 10 scallions, chopped

Combine rice wine vinegar, apple cider vinegar, and water in medium pot on medium-high heat.

Slowly whisk in sugar and salt with the vinegar mixture. Whisk thoroughly to avoid lumps and burning sugar on the bottom of the pan. Bring to a boil and remove from heat.

Combine cabbage, red onions, cilantro, and scallions in a glass or metal container (plastic may melt) and mix well.

Pour pickling liquid over cabbage mixture. Cover with an airtight cap or plastic wrap. Let stand for 30 minutes–1 hour to fully pickle.

Drain slaw and chill.

CILANTRO-LIME EMULSION

- ½ c fresh lime juice
- ¼ c rice wine vinegar
- 1 bunch cilantro with stems
- 10 scallions, trimmed and coarsely chopped
- 1 clove garlic
- 1 tsp xantham gum
- ½ c canola oil
- Salt and pepper, to taste

Puree lime juice, rice wine vinegar, cilantro, scallions, and garlic in blender until smooth.

While blender is on low, add xantham gum and blend for 30 seconds–1 minute to allow xantham gum to thicken.

Slowly add canola oil with the blender running on medium to emulsify.

Season with salt and pepper to taste.

— THE DAILY KITCHEN AND BAR —

WILD MUSHROOM BRUSCHETTA

YIELD: 4 SERVINGS

"The mushroom bruschetta was a collision," Michelle says. She had one idea; The Daily's chef had another. Customers couldn't break the tie, so eventually they pulled a few ingredients from each recipe and created a hybrid version. Both agreed, it was better than either original.

INGREDIENTS

- 3 C BALSAMIC VINEGAR
- ½ C GARLIC CLOVES
- 1 TSP + 4 TBSP VEGETABLE OIL
- 4 SPRIGS FRESH THYME
- 1 C CHÈVRE-STYLE GOAT CHEESE, SOFTENED AT ROOM TEMPERATURE
- 1 BUNCH FRESH PARSLEY
- 2 C SHIITAKE MUSHROOMS, STEMMED AND SLICED
- 2 C CREMINI MUSHROOMS, SLICED
- 1 C BROCCOLINI, CHOPPED
- 1 C CIPPOLINI ONION, CHOPPED
- 1 FRENCH BAGUETTE
- SALT AND PEPPER, TO TASTE
- 4 TBSP MICRO GREENS

INSTRUCTIONS

1. Add balsamic vinegar to a small saucepan on medium heat and bring to a simmer. Simmer until vinegar has reduced by half. Cool vinegar reduction in a large-bottomed container and put in refrigerator. It should have the consistency of honey. If it is too thick, whisk in water. If it is not thick enough, return to pot and reduce further.

2. Preheat oven to 350 degrees.

3. Coat garlic with 1 teaspoon vegetable oil and season with salt and pepper. Spread garlic on a baking sheet and roast until soft, 10–15 minutes. Allow garlic to cool. Use a mortar and pestle to mash garlic into a paste.

4. In a medium bowl, mix the leaves of 2 thyme sprigs, softened goat cheese, and garlic paste until fully combined.

5. Finely chop remaining thyme and parsley and set aside.

6. Heat a large sauté pan or wok over high heat, and add enough oil to coat the bottom of the pan. Once the oil begins to smoke, add shiitake and cremini mushrooms, broccolini, and cippolini. Reduce heat to medium low and cook until onions are soft. Remove from heat and toss with reserved herbs. Season with salt and pepper to taste.

7. Cut baguette in half horizontally, and then cut the halves in half lengthwise. This leaves you with four long pieces of baguette. Toast in oven for 3–5 minutes, or until golden brown.

8. Spread goat cheese mixture on the baguette.

9. Cut each baguette portion into 4 equal pieces and spoon cooked vegetable mixture onto each piece.

10. Drizzle with balsamic reduction and serve.

11. Garnish with micro greens.

— THE DAILY KITCHEN AND BAR —

— THE DAILY KITCHEN AND BAR —

— THE DAILY KITCHEN AND BAR —

CRISPY BRUSSELS SPROUTS WITH APPLE-LEMONGRASS GASTRIQUE

YIELD: 4–6 SERVINGS

Brussels sprouts are perfect when served with pork and game, but Michelle wanted to make something a vegan could love. That meant no bacon, no cheese, and no eggs. The key? An apple cider and lemongrass gastrique that hits all the right notes.

INGREDIENTS

- 1 STALK LEMONGRASS
- 1 C WATER
- 1 C APPLE CIDER VINEGAR
- ½ C APPLE CIDER
- 1 C SUGAR
- 4 C BRUSSELS SPROUTS
- ½ C VEGETABLE OIL
- SALT AND PEPPER, TO TASTE

INSTRUCTIONS

1. With the back of your knife, smash lemongrass thoroughly to release aromatics. Slice thinly and reserve.

2. In a medium saucepan, combine water, apple cider vinegar, and apple cider over medium heat.

3. Vigorously whisk the liquid as you slowly add sugar until the sugar has dissolved. This will keep the sugar from caking and burning to the bottom of the pan. It is not necessary for the liquid to be hot as long as it is properly mixed.

4. Add lemongrass to pot.

5. Cook on medium-low heat and reduce liquid by half, 30–45 minutes. Be careful not to reduce too far as it will thicken more as it cools. Once reduced, you can check the thickness by pouring the gastrique into a wide-based container—the larger the base the better, as this will increase cooling time—and place in refrigerator for 10 minutes. You are looking for the consistency of honey. If it's too loose, return to pan and reduce further. If it is too thick, whisk in water until you reach the desired consistency.

6. While gastrique reduces, trim base off Brussels sprouts and slice them in half, lengthwise.

7. Blanch Brussels sprouts in salted boiling water for 30 seconds and drain well. You do not want moisture on the sprouts since it will prevent searing.

8. Heat a large sauté pan to medium-high heat and cover the bottom of pan with vegetable oil. Once oil just begins to smoke, add Brussels sprouts. Do not overcrowd pan; if necessary, cook in batches. Cook until one side is browned, then flip. Once both sides are browned, drain on paper towels and season with salt and pepper to taste.

9. To plate, add cooked Brussels sprouts to a serving bowl and liberally spoon gastrique on top.

— THE DAILY KITCHEN AND BAR —

VEGGIE BURGER

YIELD: 10–16 BURGERS

Veggie burgers can be an afterthought—a basic black bean patty that serves as the standard vegetarian offering. *Michelle wanted to try something new that would satisfy a meat-eater just as much as a vegan.*

INGREDIENTS

1 C RAW, UNSALTED WALNUTS	1 C RAW, UNSALTED ALMONDS	1½ C DAIYA MOZZARELLA CHEESE	1 TSP GARLIC, MINCED
3 C RAW, UNSALTED SUNFLOWER SEEDS	1 C YELLOW ONION, CHOPPED	¼ C BRAGG AMINO ACIDS	1 TBSP BRAGG NUTRITIONAL YEAST
	1 C CANNED PINTO BEANS, DRAINED WELL	¼ C TAMARI (GLUTEN-FREE SOY SAUCE)	2–4 TBSP VEGETABLE OIL

INSTRUCTIONS

1. Puree walnuts, sunflower seeds, and almonds in a food processor in small batches until chopped as finely as possible. Empty into a large mixing bowl.

2. Puree onion, pinto beans, Daiya cheese, amino acids, tamari, garlic, and nutritional yeast in the food processor in small batches until smooth.

3. Add the bean puree to the bowl with the processed nut mix.

4. Mix everything together by hand until well combined. It should have a fairly wet consistency. Let stand for 30–45 minutes so the nuts take on some of the moisture.

5. Portion patties to desired size and press firmly so they stay together during the cooking process.

6. Heat a large saucepan over medium-high heat. Lightly cover the bottom of the pan with vegetable oil. When oil smokes lightly, add burger patties. Cook until browned, about 2 minutes per side.

— THE DAILY KITCHEN AND BAR —

CHAPTER THREE
NEIGHBORHOOD
EATS

5 RESTAURANTS

13 RECIPES

Richmond is home to many distinct neighborhoods and communities, each with their personality and charm. One of the best ways to experience them is through food. While almost every restaurant in this book can qualify as a local favorite, we've pulled out five that feel particularly well suited to represent their neck of the woods.

Whether it's in our own neighborhood or one across town, each meal at these spots gives us a new appreciation for their part of the city. And we'll keep coming back for their specialties and their specials. In their present incarnations and locations, they may not be old enough to be called "institutions," but they are well on their way.

These are the places where we long to become regulars, and where we bring our out-of-town guests to truly get a taste of what Richmond is all about.

— CHAPTER THREE: NEIGHBORHOOD EATS —

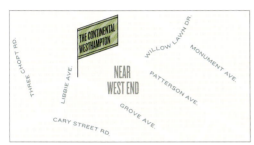

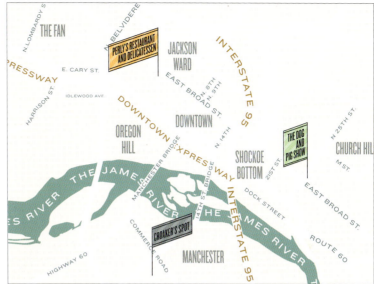

82
THE CONTINENTAL WESTHAMPTON

STUART LOWRIE

Gruyere and Prosciutto Cheese Sticks

Grilled Ribeye, Housemade Steak Sauce, Fried Onions

Sticky Toffee Pudding

92
THE DOG AND PIG SHOW

ISABEL & JAMES ECKROSH

Sweet Potato and Chorizo Hash

98
CROAKER'S SPOT

NEVERETT EGGLESTON III

Salmon Chelsea

Seafood Chili

Sweet Potato Bread Pudding

106
LUNCH. AND SUPPER!

RICK LYONS

Bacon Parmesan Brussels Sprouts

Crab Imperial Dip

From the Creek to the Cabin

114
PERLY'S RESTAURANT AND DELICATESSEN

RACHELLE & KEVIN ROBERTS

Kugel with Almond and Sunflower Crust

Veal Schnitzel Perlstein

Almond Horns

GRUYERE AND PROSCIUTTO CHEESE STICKS

GRILLED RIBEYE, HOUSEMADE STEAK SAUCE, FRIED ONIONS

STICKY TOFFEE PUDDING

THE CONTINENTAL WESTHAMPTON

THE CHEF
STUART LOWRIE

Walking into The Continental Westhampton feels a bit like stepping into a time capsule. The mint green building with aluminum accents, vintage-style posters, and other mid-century fixtures bring out a 1950s diner vibe—yet updated for a modern crowd.

The menu's designer-diner feel could be described in much the same way. There's a page on the menu dedicated to hamburgers and hotdogs (including the constantly changing daily dog), all of which can be washed down with rickeys, egg creams, milkshakes, or a root beer float.

Take a closer look and it's clear The Continental aims to be more than a greasy spoon. Club sandwiches and B.L.T.s appear next to zucchini falafel wraps and lobster paella. For the cheese sticks, chef Stuart Lowrie ditched the tepid chunk of breaded mozzarella for a prosciutto-wrapped Gruyere, fried in tempura batter.

The traditional diner steak also got an upgrade, thanks to a housemade steak sauce and beer-battered onion rings. "It's got a decent amount of ingredients in it for a steak sauce," he says. "It's got some bacon and shallots and garlic in it, some port wine, some blackberries. It's a little bit sweet and it's vinegary too."

"It's the simple idea of a steak with steak sauce and onion rings, but we tried to make the steak sauce as good as we could."

The elevated diner concept was carefully crafted by owner and restaurateur Johnny Giavos, in collaboration with Stuart and Johnny's son, Dean. "Johnny wrote a menu, and then he asked me to write a menu, and then his son Dean had several ideas," Stuart says. "We mixed them all together and came up with what we have now."

The sticky toffee pudding was one to come from Stuart's side of the menu. It's a traditional British recipe that's popular in his hometown of Edinburgh, Scotland. His mother has a bistro in northern Scotland and Stuart once spent six weeks cooking with her and her husband. "That was one of the recipes that I always wanted to learn and he showed me a good one," Stuart says. "I've been doing it ever since."

For a chef who worked his way through the ranks of Richmond country clubs, turning his focus to re-imagining dishes is a welcome shift from the scale of catering. "I worked on a lot of banquets, doing 800 crab cakes and massive displays of fruit and cheese and seafood," Stuart says. "I missed working à la carte—making an individual plate a piece of art, rather than making a display."

"It's fun being able to cook diner food, but make it upscale and a bit more fancy than your average diner."

— THE CONTINENTAL WESTHAMPTON —

WHAT WAS YOUR INTRODUCTION TO COOKING?

Working in restaurants, just washing dishes. When I was all done with my stuff, I'd help out the cooks.

WHAT ARE YOUR GO-TO INGREDIENTS?

Mirepoix, because I'm making soups and sauces every day. I go through a lot of vegetables here. I go home smelling like vegetables.

WHAT'S THE STRANGEST INGREDIENT YOU'VE EVER WORKED WITH?

It would probably be the octopus at Stella's. I'd never done it before and it's just one of those things that I guess not a lot of people are familiar with cooking.

WHAT'S YOUR FAVORITE DISH TO COOK FOR FAMILY AND FRIENDS?

I like cooking Indian food at home. It's probably my favorite food to eat. I like making a good curry. I like spicy stuff.

WHAT'S YOUR FAVORITE KITCHEN MUSIC?

I just put my iPod on shuffle. I have a lot of '80s music and British indie rock on there because that's what I grew up listening to.

— THE CONTINENTAL WESTHAMPTON —

GRUYERE AND PROSCIUTTO CHEESE STICKS

YIELD: 8 SERVINGS

How does one improve on the classic cheese stick? By wrapping it in prosciutto, deep frying it in tempura batter, and serving it with housemade marinara.

INGREDIENTS

VEGETABLE OIL FOR FRYING	3½ OZ PROSCIUTTO	1 C TEMPURA BATTER (RECIPE PG. 86)	8 OZ MARINARA (RECIPE PG. 86)
8 OZ GRUYERE	3 TBSP CORNSTARCH	MIXED GREENS OR MICRO HERBS	

SPECIAL EQUIPMENT

TOOTHPICKS

CONTINUES ON NEXT PAGE

— THE CONTINENTAL WESTHAMPTON —

TEMPURA BATTER

| 1 c all-purpose flour | 2 Tbsp cornstarch | ½ tsp salt | ½ tsp baking powder | 1¼ c soda water |

Mix together all dry ingredients. Whisk in soda water until batter is smooth.

HOUSEMADE MARINARA

2 Tbsp olive oil	1 c red wine	1 Tbsp fresh oregano, chopped
½ Spanish onion, chopped	16 oz canned tomatoes	1 tsp crushed red pepper
1 small carrot, chopped	2 Tbsp tomato paste	½ tsp sugar
1 rib celery, chopped	1 Tbsp fresh basil, chopped	Salt and pepper, to taste
8 cloves garlic, minced		

In a large saucepan, heat olive oil over medium-high heat and add onion, carrot, and celery. Cook until vegetables are tender and have caramelized, about 8 minutes. Be careful not to burn; reduce heat to medium if mixture starts browning too quickly.

Add garlic and cook for an additional 1–2 minutes.

Add red wine to the pot and simmer until reduced by half.

Add all remaining ingredients and cook for 20 minutes.

Puree sauce in batches in a blender or with an immersion blender.

INSTRUCTIONS

1. Preheat a deep fryer or a large pot full of oil to 350 degrees.

2. Cut Gruyere into 1-ounce, finger-sized sticks.

3. Shave prosciutto into paper-thin slices. Wrap cheese sticks with prosciutto and skewer through with a toothpick to secure the meat.

4. Dust in cornstarch, shaking off excess.

5. Dip in tempura batter and carefully drop into fryer or pot. Fry for about 2 minutes and remove.

6. Remove toothpicks and serve on a bed of mixed greens or garnish with micro herbs. Serve with marinara dipping sauce.

— THE CONTINENTAL WESTHAMPTON —

RIBEYE STEAK WITH HOUSEMADE STEAK SAUCE AND TEMPURA ONION RINGS

YIELD: 4 SERVINGS

This isn't your traditional diner steak, although Stuart Lowrie says that was definitely the starting point. The sweet and vinegary steak sauce—made with bacon and blackberries—makes all the difference.

INGREDIENTS

- 4 RIBEYE STEAKS, ABOUT 1¼- TO 1½-INCH THICK
- 1½ TBSP BUTTER
- 1½ TBSP VEGETABLE OIL
- OIL FOR FRYING
- 2 SWEET ONIONS, SLICED INTO ½-INCH RINGS
- TEMPURA BATTER (RECIPE PG. 86)
- 1 C HOUSEMADE STEAK SAUCE (RECIPE PG. 89)
- SALT AND PEPPER, TO TASTE

INSTRUCTIONS

Cook steaks

1. Bring steaks to room temperature and pat dry with a paper towel.
2. Liberally season both sides of the steaks with salt and pepper.
3. Heat butter and vegetable oil in a large cast-iron skillet over medium-high heat.
4. Cook steaks for about 4 minutes per side for medium rare (internal temperature of 135 degrees), or until desired doneness.
5. Transfer steaks to a cutting board and let rest for up to 5 minutes before serving.

Fry onion rings

1. Preheat a deep fryer or a large pot full of oil to 350 degrees.
2. Dip onion rings in tempura batter, gently shaking off excess.
3. Fry onions until golden brown, then drain them on paper towels. Immediately season with salt.

Assemble

» Top each steak with onion rings and serve with about ¼ cup housemade steak sauce. We serve this dish with mashed potatoes and seasonal vegetables at the restaurant.

— THE CONTINENTAL WESTHAMPTON —

CONTINENTAL STEAK SAUCE

- 5 bacon strips, finely chopped
- 5 garlic cloves, minced
- 2 shallots, minced
- ½ c blackberries
- 1 c port wine
- ¾ c tamarind juice
- ⅓ c ketchup
- ½ c Worcestershire sauce
- ½ c Cholula hot sauce
- 2 Tbsp brown sugar
- 1 juniper berry

In a large skillet, cook bacon over medium-high heat until browned.

Add garlic, shallots, and blackberries. Cook until shallots are translucent, about 2 minutes.

Add port and bring to a boil. Simmer for about 5 minutes, reducing the port.

Add all other ingredients and return to a boil. Reduce to a simmer and cook for 20 minutes.

Remove juniper berry and store sauce in refrigerator in an airtight container.

— THE CONTINENTAL WESTHAMPTON —

— THE CONTINENTAL WESTHAMPTON —

STICKY TOFFEE PUDDING WITH SALTED CARAMEL SAUCE

YIELD: 16 SERVINGS

Toffee pudding is a traditional British dessert that is unfamiliar to most Americans, but is well worth getting acquainted with. It's the original gooey bar. Stuart serves his pudding with vanilla ice cream, but also suggests a homemade whipped cream or English double cream.

Ingredients

- 12 OZ DATES
- 4 OZ GOLDEN RAISINS
- 1 LB BUTTER
- 1 LB DARK BROWN SUGAR
- 1 TSP VANILLA EXTRACT
- ½ TSP SALT
- 1 TBSP BAKING POWDER
- 6 EGGS
- 1 LB FLOUR
- SALTED CARAMEL SAUCE (RECIPE BELOW)
- MINT

SALTED CARAMEL SAUCE

- 2 c sugar
- 2 Tbsp water
- ½ qt heavy cream
- ¼ tsp sea salt

In a medium pot, add sugar and water and bring to a boil. Cook until sugar starts to brown.

When sugar has caramelized and is a rich golden brown, pour in heavy cream. Return to a boil and reduce to a simmer. Cook for about 5 minutes. Add sea salt. Taste the sauce and add more salt if you like.

INSTRUCTIONS

1. In a large bowl, barely cover dates and raisins with hot water. Soak overnight.
2. Preheat oven to 345 degrees.
3. Drain soaked fruit and puree in a food processor, leaving it a little chunky. Set aside.
4. In a mixer, cream butter and brown sugar. Mix in vanilla, salt, and baking powder.
5. With mixer on slow, add eggs and flour little by little, periodically scraping down the sides of the bowl.
6. Fold in pureed dates and raisins.
7. Pour batter into a lined cake pan and bake for 1 hour–1 hour 20 minutes. Cool overnight. Cut into serving portions.
8. Ladle 2–3 tablespoons of salted caramel sauce over each portion of the cold pudding and microwave 1–2 minutes to warm. Serve with an additional drizzle of salted caramel sauce, a scoop of vanilla ice cream, and a sprig of mint.

THE DOG AND PIG SHOW

PROPRIETOR

ISABEL ECKROSH

CHEF & PROPRIETOR

JAMES ECKROSH

Soon after moving to Richmond in late 2013, James and Isabel Eckrosh began working to open a food truck. A commissary kitchen proved hard to find, but the two found an alternate plan in an unlikely place—a yard sale in their new neighborhood of Church Hill.

The sale was at a catering company where the two had stopped to look for cooking supplies. They struck up a conversation with the owner and learned she was closing up shop. While the kitchen wasn't equipped for a full-scale restaurant, James and Isabel still saw potential.

"I think James really liked the renegade style of a food truck," Isabel says. "Then we found this spot and thought, we'll do it here. It will be like a food truck that doesn't move."

A small kitchen may mean a small menu, but no one could argue it's holding them back.

From their sunny takeout shop on 25th Street, James turns out shrimp and grits with kimchi and bacon butter, and a rich grilled cheese made with Muenster, pimento cheese, and tomato jam. Isabel keeps the front counter stocked with a selection of desserts like moon pies and salted chocolate chip cookies.

"We'll change things up," Isabel says. "But we know we do these well."

They show off their full range once a month at Sunday Suppers held in their Church Hill home. Limited to 12 friends, neighbors, and strangers, James cooks up a Southern- and Asian-inspired menu with dishes like sweet potato and chorizo hash.

The dish is built on a corned beef and Andouille sausage hash he made while working for a restaurant in New Orleans. He changed the recipe when cooking dinner for friends, using

RECIPE

SWEET POTATO AND CHORIZO HASH

the chorizo he had on hand. Sometimes he tops it with eggs or adds spinach. Sometimes he mixes in pork belly.

However it's prepared, the hash, just like everything at The Dog and Pig Show, is meant to be served with good friends and lively conversation.

"Food is a connecting thing," Isabel says. "It brings people together. That's something I think is very fun for our suppers. Everyone ends up hanging out and laughing and enjoying themselves."

— THE DOG AND PIG SHOW —

"Food is a connecting thing."

—Isabel Eckrosh

WHAT ARE YOUR GO-TO INGREDIENTS?

James: Pork is number one. I would say pork, bacon, and butter.

WHERE DO YOU GO OUT TO EAT?

Isabel: Metzger. I love their date night. It's perfect. And The Rogue Gentlemen for drinks. They do a great job with their cocktails.

WHAT'S THE STRANGEST INGREDIENT YOU'VE EVER WORKED WITH?

James: Beet sorbet. I had to make it with liquid nitrogen.

WHAT'S YOUR FAVORITE DISH TO COOK FOR FAMILY AND FRIENDS?

James: Asian noodles, because I like it. That's my major motivator.

WHAT'S YOUR FAVORITE KITCHEN MUSIC?

James: Either metal or hip-hop.

Isabel: I'd say Beyonce.

James: You can't put all three of those. I can't walk into Comfort and look at all those ax murderers in that kitchen and they're like, "oh, you listen to Beyonce, yeah?"

— THE DOG AND PIG SHOW —

SWEET POTATO AND CHORIZO HASH

YIELD: 6 SERVINGS

This dish has evolved over family holidays and dinners with friends. James Eckrosh has prepared it with corned beef, Andouille sausage, and pork belly instead of the chorizo. Or top it with scrambled eggs for breakfast the next morning.

CONTINUES ON NEXT PAGE

— THE DOG AND PIG SHOW —

IN THE KITCHEN WITH JAMES ECKROSH | SWEET POTATO AND CHORIZO HASH

INGREDIENTS

- 3–4 LARGE SWEET POTATOES, PEELED AND CUT INTO 1–1½-INCH CUBES
- 3½ TBSP BUTTER OR BACON FAT, MELTED + 1 TSP TO GREASE ROASTING PAN
- 1–2 LBS FRESH CHORIZO (NOT THE DRIED AND CURED VARIETY), CASINGS REMOVED
- 2 LARGE RED ONIONS, DICED
- 3–4 POBLANO OR BELL PEPPERS, SEEDED, MEMBRANES REMOVED, AND DICED
- 3 TBSP GARLIC, MINCED
- KOSHER SALT AND FRESHLY GROUND PEPPER, TO TASTE

INSTRUCTIONS

PREPARE POTATOES

1. Preheat oven to 300 degrees.
2. Toss potatoes with 2 tablespoons melted butter or bacon fat.
3. Spread onto a large foil-lined baking sheet and place in oven.
4. Cook for 30–45 minutes. Potatoes will cook differently depending on the oven, water content of potatoes, and size of the cubes, so check frequently and as soon as they begin to soften, remove from oven. Do not overcook.
5. Grease a large roasting pan with butter or bacon fat and transfer cooked potatoes.

COOK CHORIZO

1. In a large sauté pan, heat ½ tablespoon of butter or bacon fat over medium heat until hot.
2. Break up chorizo with your hands and add to pan. Continue to break up the meat with a spoon. Be sure not to stir too much to allow the chorizo to brown.
3. When chorizo is cooked, raise heat to high for additional browning. Cook for 2 more minutes, being careful not to burn.

— THE DOG AND PIG SHOW —

IN THE KITCHEN WITH JAMES ECKROSH | SWEET POTATO AND CHORIZO HASH

4. Remove pan from heat and drain most excess fat. Leaving a little fat is okay since it adds flavor to the hash.

5. Transfer chorizo to roasting pan with potatoes.

SAUTÉ ONIONS AND PEPPERS

1. Heat 1 tablespoon butter or bacon fat in large sauté pan over medium-high heat until hot.

2. Add onions and peppers and reduce heat to medium low. Cook peppers and onions until soft but not browned, about 10 minutes.

3. Return to medium-high heat and stir until onions and peppers begin to brown, adding a bit more butter or bacon fat if necessary.

4. When onions and peppers are mostly brown add minced garlic and stir for about 2 minutes, being careful not to burn the garlic.

5. Remove from heat and transfer to roasting pan with the potatoes and chorizo.

FINISH THE HASH

1. Preheat oven to 400 degrees.

2. Toss all ingredients in the roasting pan until well mixed. Taste seasoning of mixture and season with kosher salt and freshly ground pepper to taste.

3. Place roasting pan on middle rack and cook for 10–15 minutes.

4. Switch oven to broil and cook an additional 5–10 minutes, or longer if necessary, until top of hash begins to brown. Serve.

VARIATIONS:

This hash is delicious on its own or topped with eggs, sautéed baby spinach, or fresh herbs, such as flat leaf parsley, cilantro, or scallions. For a really decadent meal, serve it with a rich and tangy hollandaise sauce. We love eating our leftover hash with fried eggs, hot sauce, and chimichurri sauce.

CROAKER'S SPOT

The legend of Mr. Croaker begins in Jackson Ward where he grew up. After graduating from Armstrong High School, he moved to New York and befriended the artists, writers, jazz musicians, and entrepreneurs living in Harlem. He wasn't a musician, but joined many jazz musicians on tour in the South, always seeking out the best soul food restaurants. Starting his own restaurant seemed inevitable and just as the Harlem Renaissance was taking off, Croaker's opened its doors as a late-night destination for the local artist community.

Neverett Eggleston III's story begins in much the same way. His grandfather opened Eggleston Hotel on the corner of Second and Leigh streets in Jackson Ward—also known as the Harlem of the South. Neverett grew up working in the hotel and took over the business from his father. He eventually closed the hotel in the late '90s to open his own restaurant—Croaker's Spot—across the street. The restaurant is inspired by the story of Mr. Croaker, whom Neverett met when Mr. Croaker returned to Richmond in his later years.

Musicians may have swarmed the original Croaker's for late-night soul food with fellow artists, but customers line up in Richmond for the signature fish boat—fried fish filets served with peppers and onions, special sauce, sweet corn bread, and potatoes.

"There's no Croaker's Spot without the fish boat," says Enjoli Moon, communications director for Croaker's Spot. She's quick to point out, however, that Croaker's Spot is much more than a fish house. They also serve up made-from-scratch seafood dishes like the seafood chili—a hearty soup of scallops, shrimp and fish simmered with fresh vegetables—and grilled salmon with kielbasa sausage and sautéed shrimp in a Cajun cream sauce.

After 10 years in Jackson Ward, Neverett moved Croaker's Spot to Hull Street, on the edge of Old Manchester, in 2011. The new space not only doubled the capacity, but is also a chance to continue a celebration of black culture and

RECIPES

SALMON CHELSEA

SEAFOOD CHILI

SWEET POTATO BREAD PUDDING

PROPRIETOR

NEVERETT EGGLESTON III

contributions that's been a part of Croaker's Spot from the very beginning.

"The historical relevance of Jackson Ward and Old Manchester is really important," Enjoli says. "The spaces that he chooses have had some connection to black excellence on a historical level. Being in Jackson Ward initially he was trying to recapture what Second Street was in its heyday. He wants to create spaces where black life and black history could be celebrated."

— CROAKER'S SPOT —

SALMON CHELSEA

YIELD: 1 SERVING

This dish is Southern comfort food—plain and simple. Salmon, sausage, and shrimp come together as if they were made for each other. This dish is served with rice at the restaurant but would pair just as well with pasta.

INGREDIENTS

- 1 TBSP VEGETABLE OIL
- 8 OZ SALMON FILET, SKIN REMOVED
- 2 OZ KIELBASA SAUSAGE, DICED
- 4–5 MEDIUM–LARGE SHRIMP, PEELED AND DEVEINED
- ¾ C HEAVY CREAM
- 1½ TSP CAJUN OR BLACKENING SEASONING
- ⅓ C SCALLIONS, FINELY CHOPPED
- ⅓ C TOMATOES, DICED
- ½ C PARMESAN CHEESE, SHREDDED

INSTRUCTIONS

1. Add vegetable oil to sauté pan over medium-high heat. When pan is very hot, add salmon. Cook until golden brown, 2–3 minutes per side. Internal temperature should be 145 degrees. Remove fish from pan and set aside. Discard oil.

2. Reheat the same pan over medium-high heat and add kielbasa. Cook for 1–2 minutes. Add shrimp and cook for additional 1 minute.

3. Add heavy cream, Cajun seasoning, scallions, and tomatoes and simmer for 3–5 minutes or until sauce has thickened.

4. Add Parmesan to sauce and stir until thick, about 1 minute.

5. To finish, pour sauce over cooked salmon. Serve with rice and seasonal vegetables.

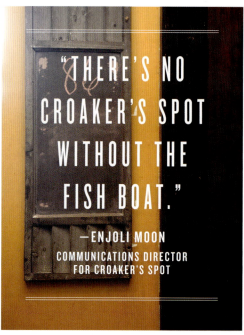

"THERE'S NO CROAKER'S SPOT WITHOUT THE FISH BOAT."

—ENJOLI MOON
COMMUNICATIONS DIRECTOR FOR CROAKER'S SPOT

— CROAKER'S SPOT —

— CROAKER'S SPOT —

SEAFOOD CHILI

YIELD: 6 SERVINGS

Seafood Chili is one of the most popular dishes at Croaker's Spot. "It's something we haven't seen duplicated anywhere else—at least not the way we do it," says Enjoli Moon, communications director. "It shows our personality."

INGREDIENTS

- 2 TBSP + 1 TBSP VEGETABLE OIL
- 4 OZ KIDNEY BEANS
- 1 RED PEPPER, CHOPPED
- 1 GREEN PEPPER, CHOPPED
- 1 OZ CARROTS, SHREDDED
- ½ RED ONION, DICED
- 2 OZ TOMATO PASTE
- 5 OZ TOMATOES, DICED
- 1 TBSP CRAB BASE
- 2 TBSP CHILI POWDER
- 2 TBSP GROUND CUMIN
- 1–2 C WATER
- 3 OZ BAY SCALLOPS
- 3 OZ SHRIMP, DICED
- 3 OZ FISH OF YOUR CHOICE, CHOPPED

OPTIONAL CHILI TOPPINGS:

- SHREDDED CHEESE
- SLICED JALAPEÑO
- DICED RED ONION
- SLICED GREEN ONION
- BANANA PEPPERS

INSTRUCTIONS

1. In a medium saucepan, heat 2 tablespoons vegetable oil over medium-high heat. Add kidney beans, peppers, carrots, onion, tomato paste, and tomatoes. Cook for 5–10 minutes until the vegetables start to brown.

2. Add crab base, chili powder, and cumin to the cooked vegetables and mix until well incorporated.

3. Add just enough water to cover vegetables. Bring to a simmer.

4. While sauce simmers, heat a separate sauté pan with remaining 1 tablespoon vegetable oil over medium-high heat. Add scallops, shrimp, and fish and cook for 3–5 minutes until seafood is opaque.

5. Add seafood to chili sauce and simmer for 8–10 minutes. If chili gets too thick, add a little water until it is desired consistency.

6. Serve with your favorite toppings.

— CROAKER'S SPOT —

SWEET POTATO BREAD PUDDING

Sweet potatoes have been relegated to the holiday season for far too long. This bread pudding is delicious year-round.

The lemon brightens the dessert and balances out the cinnamon and nutmeg.

YIELD: 12 SERVINGS

Ingredients

- 1 TSP BUTTER, OIL, OR COOKING SPRAY TO GREASE PAN
- 1 LOAF WHITE BREAD (ABOUT 22 SLICES), TOASTED AND CUT INTO 1-INCH CUBES
- 2 MEDIUM BOILED SWEET POTATOES, PEELED AND CUT INTO ¼-INCH SLICES
- 8 EGGS
- 2 TSP CINNAMON
- 1 TBSP NUTMEG
- 3 C GRANULATED SUGAR
- 1 TBSP VANILLA EXTRACT
- 1 TSP LEMON EXTRACT
- 4 C HALF-AND-HALF
- 2 C POWDERED SUGAR
- ¼ C LEMON JUICE

INSTRUCTIONS

1. Preheat oven to 325 degrees. Grease 13x9-inch baking pan.
2. Line pan with a layer of bread cubes. Cover bread with a layer of sweet potato slices. Continue alternating layers until you have used all of the bread and sweet potato.
3. In a large bowl, beat eggs with cinnamon, nutmeg, granulated sugar, and vanilla and lemon extracts. Slowly beat half-and-half into egg mixture.
4. Pour liquid over bread and sweet potatoes in the baking pan.
5. Bake for 1 hour or until a knife inserted into the center of the pudding comes out clean.
6. While bread pudding bakes, prepare the glaze. In a medium bowl, mix powdered sugar and lemon juice until smooth.
7. Pour glaze over finished bread pudding. Serve warm.

Rick Lyons

When Rick Lyons rolled into town in the early '90s to visit his brother, it only took a weekend for him to ditch the City of Brotherly Love for some Southern hospitality. He went back to Philadelphia that Monday, packed up his stuff, and by Monday night, Richmond was home.

"Everybody held the door for you, everybody said please and thank you, and how are you, and I'm like… what's wrong with these people?" he says. "I did a little soul searching and said, this place is cool. I like it here."

Rick soon met James Talley who was opening Memphis Bar and Grill in Shockoe Bottom. A carpenter by trade, Rick offered to help build out the bar and then run it.

Talley took him up on the offer and over the years, Rick made a career opening, owning,

LUNCH. AND SUPPER!

 **RECIPES** | **BACON PARMESAN BRUSSELS SPROUTS** | **CRAB IMPERIAL DIP** | **FROM THE CREEK TO THE CABIN**

and operating Richmond bar staples like Star-lite Dining and Lounge and Bandito's Burrito Lounge.

But after 13 years of slinging drinks until 2 a.m., he was ready for a change.

One day, he was driving around his neighborhood in Scott's Addition when he noticed Sue's Country Kitchen was for sale. "After spending a few days with the sweetest owners in the world," he says, "we all came to an agreement and they decided I'd be the best fit to take over the building."

Again, Rick built the space by hand and after eight months, Lunch. was open for business. "I was able to cut my teeth at Lunch.," he says. "It was small enough that I could put my hands on everything—guide it and control it and get it to where I wanted it to be."

After settling into a groove at Lunch., the space next door became available and Rick was ready to expand with Supper!

"It's cool because it keeps Lunch. as Lunch.," he says. "It's 25 seats and you get comfy cozy. Supper! is only 45 seats, which continues that trend but gives us the room to get out there on a larger scale."

Both Lunch. and Supper! feature menus of Southern staples, but Rick is also aware that it takes more than fluffy mashed potatoes and cheesy grits to keep people coming back. That's why you'll find anything from breakfast sandwiches on huge buttermilk biscuits to bacon Parmesan Brussels sprouts to rainbow trout with smoked tomato coulis.

"We're really versatile here and our customers are eclectic," he says. "You've got to have faith in a restaurant that they know what they're doing. That's something we strive for, to create that culture that says, we got it. We know what we're doing."

— LUNCH. AND SUPPER! —

"EVERYBODY HELD THE DOOR FOR YOU, EVERYBODY SAID PLEASE AND THANK YOU, AND HOW ARE YOU, AND I'M LIKE... WHAT'S WRONG WITH THESE PEOPLE? I DID A LITTLE SOUL SEARCHING AND SAID, THIS PLACE IS COOL. I LIKE IT HERE."

— RICK LYONS

WHAT ARE YOUR GO-TO INGREDIENTS?

Bacon. Well, technically I would say my go-to ingredient would be bacon grease. We call it the golden liquid. It could pretty much go in anything and make it taste better.

WHAT'S THE STRANGEST INGREDIENT YOU'VE EVER WORKED WITH?

Pacu fish ribs. They come in packed like ribs, we cook 'em like ribs, and they pull off, just like eating ribs. Of course, they're small, so it's like nibbling on little bones.

WHERE DO YOU GO OUT TO EAT?

The Magpie.

WHAT'S YOUR FAVORITE KITCHEN MUSIC?

Katy Perry radio! We rock it back there. It puts a whole pep in your step, gets us moving back there. Our food tastes good because of Katy Perry. All that delicious flavor bleeds through Katy Perry.

WHAT'S THE LAST MEAL YOU MADE FOR YOURSELF?

Oatmeal out of a box. That's what I ate this morning.

WHAT WAS YOUR INTRODUCTION TO COOKING?

Johnny Giavos and Sidewalk Café.

— LUNCH. AND SUPPER! —

BACON PARMESAN BRUSSELS SPROUTS

YIELD: 2 SERVINGS

Brussels sprouts are all the rage, but at Lunch. and Supper!, they know that the best way to prepare them is with a little bacon, onion, and butter. The key is getting a good sear, then reducing the heat to make sure the Brussels sprouts have a chance to become tender.

INGREDIENTS

- 3 TBSP BACON FAT
- 2 C BRUSSELS SPROUTS, BOTTOMS TRIMMED AND QUARTERED
- 1/3 C RED ONION, THINLY SLICED
- 1 TBSP BUTTER
- 4 SLICES BACON, COOKED AND CRUMBLED
- SMOKED SALT AND PEPPER, TO TASTE
- 3 TBSP FRESH PARMESAN, GRATED

INSTRUCTIONS

1. Heat bacon fat in a cast-iron skillet over medium-high heat. Sauté Brussels sprouts and red onion until Brussels are starting to sear, 3–5 minutes
2. Reduce heat to medium and add butter and bacon crumbles. Continue to sauté until Brussels are tender, 6–10 minutes
3. Add smoked salt and pepper to taste. Sprinkle with Parmesan and serve.

— LUNCH. AND SUPPER! —

CRAB IMPERIAL DIP

YIELD: 4–6 SERVINGS

This crab dip is distinguished by jumbo lump crabmeat, pickled jalapeños, and smoked salt. This popular appetizer is served with a hearty portion of toasty pita bread and some lemon. It's so good, it's hard not to eat the whole batch.

Ingredients

- 12 OZ CREAM CHEESE
- ½ C HEAVY CREAM
- ½ LB CRABMEAT (LUMP CRAB PREFERRED)
- ½ C ARTICHOKE HEARTS, DICED
- ¼ C PICKLED JALAPEÑOS, DICED
- 1 C SHREDDED PARMESAN
- SMOKED SALT AND PEPPER, TO TASTE
- ⅛ C PANKO BREADCRUMBS
- 1 TBSP MICRO GREENS
- ½ LEMON

INSTRUCTIONS

1. Heat a large nonstick skillet over low heat. Add cream cheese and heavy cream. Let cream cheese melt completely.
2. Add all remaining ingredients, except panko, one at a time and slowly blend everything together.
3. Cook on low heat for 30 minutes to let the flavors meld.
4. Preheat broiler. Transfer the dip to an ovenproof dish, top with panko, and broil for 5 minutes or until golden brown. Serve immediately.
5. Garnish with micro greens and serve with lemon and pita bread.

— LUNCH. AND SUPPER! —

FROM THE CREEK TO THE CABIN
CAST-IRON RAINBOW TROUT OVER CHEESE GRITS AND TOPPED WITH SMOKED TOMATO COULIS

YIELD: 2 SERVINGS

While everyone else in town is making shrimp and grits, at Lunch. and Supper!, cheese grits are topped with rainbow trout. The smoked tomato coulis adds a touch of sweetness and acidity to brighten the dish. The smoke flavor is subtle, but present, adding yet another dimension.

INGREDIENTS

- 12 OZ ITALIAN PLUM TOMATOES, WHOLE
- 2 TBSP OLIVE OIL
- ⅔ C YELLOW ONION, FINELY DICED
- ⅔ C CARROTS, FINELY DICED
- 1 TBSP BLACKENED SEASONING
- 1 C BYRD MILL WHITE GRITS
- 4 C WATER
- 2 TBSP + 2 TBSP BUTTER
- 4 OZ CHEDDAR CHEESE
- SMOKED SALT AND PEPPER, TO TASTE
- 2 8-OZ TROUT FILETS, SKIN ON
- 2 TBSP MICRO GREENS

INSTRUCTIONS

Prepare tomato coulis

1. Place tomatoes in a smoker on low heat for 15–20 minutes. Set aside and let cool. If a smoker is not available, simmer the coulis for 10 minutes before serving. This will give the coulis a stronger blackened flavor.

2. Heat olive oil in a large sauté pan over medium heat. Cook onions and carrots until tender, about 10 minutes. Place in a large bowl.

3. Crush smoked tomatoes by hand and add to bowl.

4. Sprinkle in your favorite blackened seasoning and mix thoroughly.

Prepare grits

1. Mix grits and water in a pot. Bring to a boil, then reduce to a simmer.

— LUNCH. AND SUPPER! —

2. Simmer for about 45 minutes or until the grits are tender, stirring frequently.
3. Add 2 tablespoons butter and cheese to the pot and mix until melted.
4. Add smoked salt and pepper to taste.

Cook trout

1. Preheat oven to broil.
2. Season both sides of trout with smoked salt and pepper.
3. Melt 2 tablespoons butter in a cast-iron skillet over medium-high heat. Place fish skin-side down and sear for 1–2 minutes.
4. Flip fish over and place in oven. Broil for about 5 minutes. Remove when fish is fully cooked and has an internal temperature of 145 degrees.

Assemble

1. To serve, add 1½ cups cheese grits to a plate. Place a trout filet over grits and top with ⅓ cup tomato coulis.
2. Garnish with micro greens.

PERLY'S RESTAURANT AND DELICATESSEN

| KUGEL WITH ALMOND AND SUNFLOWER CRUST | VEAL SCHNITZEL PERLSTEIN | ALMOND HORNS |

Kevin Roberts was at the bank when he noticed a sign on a building across the street. "To my dear friends," it read. "Perly's has hit a rough patch. I am hoping to sort it out but must close for now." A few days later, the downtown fixture for more than 50 years closed for good, much to the shock of Richmonders.

The timing was serendipitous. Kevin's first restaurant, The Black Sheep, was running smoothly and he was looking for the right space to open a traditional New York Jewish delicatessen rooted in his wife Rachelle's family recipes. His search led him as far as Charlottesville, but after seeing that sign on the window, Kevin knew immediately that Perly's was just what he was looking for.

Expectations were high. In the *Richmond Times-Dispatch*, Karri Peifer wrote, "Everyone's been waiting with bated breath to see who would claim the coveted downtown spot."

Kevin doesn't deny it was daunting to take over a Richmond landmark, but at the same time, knew many were just happy to see the doors open again. "It's helpful," he says, "to have a place that already has a following, a reputation. It's a Richmond mainstay."

Kevin and Rachelle preserved much of the space's art deco style, ensuring that it wouldn't feel foreign to longtime patrons. They added a marble bar top, a few booths, and lined the walls with photos of Rachelle's ancestors.

Rachelle's family was also an influence on the menu, which features potato latkes, beef knish, lokshen kugel, and matzoh ball soup. Many of the traditional recipes were taken up a notch, such as the matzoh brei—a basic dish of matzoh, eggs, and a dollop of grape jelly. Kevin's version adds green onions, apples, and cheddar, and swaps the jelly for a tomato-plum jam.

"My mom is very into ancestry and genealogy, and I think it's very important to her to keep alive these traditions and recipes from the old country and from ancestors," Rachelle says. "It's exciting to see these things that were such a big part of my childhood, and to see people who have never had it before enjoying it."

CO-OWNER

RACHELLE ROBERTS

CHEF & CO-OWNER

KEVIN ROBERTS

Some still miss the former landmark. "We still have people call and ask if we serve biscuits," Kevin says. "We're like, yeah, but they're round and they have cream cheese on them."

But many are flocking to Perly's to find something new in the familiar. "It might be a word someone is unfamiliar with, like the kugel or the knish," Kevin says. "But the knish is nothing more than mashed potatoes wrapped in pastry; it's a pot pie. I think that's one of the things that drew me—it's comfort food."

— PERLY'S RESTAURANT AND DELICATESSEN —

"IT'S HELPFUL TO HAVE A PLACE THAT ALREADY HAS A FOLLOWING, A REPUTATION. IT'S A RICHMOND MAINSTAY."

—KEVIN ROBERTS

"IT'S EXCITING TO SEE THESE THINGS THAT WERE SUCH A BIG PART OF MY CHILDHOOD, AND TO SEE PEOPLE WHO HAVE NEVER HAD IT BEFORE ENJOYING IT."

—RACHELLE ROBERTS

WHAT ARE YOUR GO-TO INGREDIENTS?

Kevin: At the restaurant: Dill, salmon, and schmaltz.
At home: Eggs, cereal, almond milk, fruit.

WHAT'S YOUR FAVORITE DISH TO COOK FOR FAMILY AND FRIENDS?

Rachelle: I have a couple go-to dishes. My favorite thing to make is lokshen kugel. I love making that because usually no one's had it.

WHERE DO YOU GO OUT TO EAT?

Kevin: Metzger, Dutch & Co., Morris St. Café.

Rachelle: Mostly it's Morris St. Café breakfast. We love to eat breakfast. That's our favorite thing is to find places to eat good breakfast.

WHAT'S THE STRANGEST INGREDIENT YOU'VE EVER WORKED WITH?

Kevin: Turtle.

WHAT'S YOUR FAVORITE KITCHEN MUSIC?

Kevin: I'm a sucker for '70s soft rock. It's just what was just engrained in my brain when I was growing up and my parents had it on in the car. It puts me in a good mood. It's not overbearing.

Rachelle: Podcasts and NPR.

WHAT WAS YOUR INTRODUCTION TO COOKING?

Kevin: I was a dishwasher at the Bamboo Café on Mulberry. I was going to VCU. I had to fill in for a guy one night. I just started cooking, and had fun doing it.

Rachelle: I decided I was going to be a vegetarian a long time ago and was forced to learn how to cook for myself because my mom was not going to be cooking vegetarian meals for me.

— PERLY'S RESTAURANT AND DELICATESSEN —

"WE STILL HAVE PEOPLE CALL AND ASK IF WE SERVE BISCUITS... WE'RE LIKE, YEAH, BUT THEY'RE ROUND AND THEY HAVE CREAM CHEESE ON THEM."
—KEVIN ROBERTS

— PERLY'S RESTAURANT AND DELICATESSEN —

KUGEL WITH ALMOND AND SUNFLOWER CRUST

YIELD: 16 SERVINGS

Kugel is a traditional Jewish casserole made with egg noodles or potatoes, but from there, the flavors run the gamut from sweet to savory. Perly's rendition starts with roasted cauliflower that is pureed into the custard base. It's topped with a crunchy combination of sunflower seeds and almonds.

INGREDIENTS

- 1 HEAD CAULIFLOWER
- 2 TBSP VEGETABLE OIL
- 1 C MILK
- 1 LB EGG NOODLES
- 1 LEEK
- 2 TBSP + 2 TBSP + 2 TBSP BUTTER, MELTED
- 2 TSP FRESH THYME, CHOPPED
- 8 EGGS
- ½ C SOUR CREAM
- 1 TBSP SALT
- 1 TSP WHITE PEPPER
- ½ C SLIVERED ALMONDS
- ½ C SUNFLOWER SEEDS
- 2 TBSP FRESH PARSLEY, CHOPPED
- ½ C PANKO BREADCRUMBS
- SALT AND PEPPER, TO TASTE

INSTRUCTIONS

1. Preheat oven to 400 degrees. Chop cauliflower into small florets and toss with vegetable oil. Bake for 25–30 minutes until cauliflower is soft and starts to brown. Transfer half of roasted cauliflower to a food processor and puree with milk until smooth. Reduce oven temperature to 350 degrees.

2. Boil egg noodles according to package instructions. Drain and cool.

3. Cut off tough green portion of the leek and clean white portion thoroughly (there is a lot of grit between layers). Cut in half lengthwise, then cut into thin slices against the grain.

4. Melt 2 tablespoons of butter in a skillet over medium-low heat. Sauté leeks and thyme until leeks are translucent, but do not have any color.

5. In a large bowl, beat together leek mixture, 2 tablespoons melted butter, eggs, sour cream, salt, and pepper. Fold in roasted cauliflower florets, cauliflower puree, and noodles.

6. Prepare topping by mixing together 2 tablespoons melted butter, slivered almonds, sunflower seeds, parsley, and panko breadcrumbs. Add salt and pepper to taste.

7. Grease a large ovenproof dish and fill with kugel. Top with the almond-sunflower mixture and bake for 45 minutes–1 hour.

— PERLY'S RESTAURANT AND DELICATESSEN —

— PERLY'S RESTAURANT AND DELICATESSEN —

VEAL SCHNITZEL PERLSTEIN

YIELD: 4 SERVINGS

Named for the original owners at Perly's, this dish is Kevin Roberts's take on the classic lemon and caper veal schnitzel.

Ultra-crispy panko-crusted veal is topped with sunny side up eggs and brightened with a roasted fennel and parsley salad.

INGREDIENTS

- 2 FENNEL BULBS
- 2 TBSP OLIVE OIL
- 1 TSP SALT
- ½ TSP PEPPER
- ½ C APPLE CIDER VINEGAR
- 1½ TBSP SUGAR
- ¼ C RED ONION, THINLY SLICED
- 4 ROMA TOMATOES OR 1 LARGE RIPE TOMATO, PEELED, SEEDED, AND DICED
- 4 C ITALIAN FLAT LEAF PARSLEY, STEMMED
- 3 TBSP CAPERS
- 3 OZ SMOKED TROUT, ROUGHLY CHOPPED OR TORN INTO BITE-SIZED PIECES
- 3 TBSP PRESERVED LEMON VINAIGRETTE (RECIPE PG. 122)
- 4 + 8 EGGS
- 3 C SEASONED FLOUR OR CHICKEN BREADER (PRE-SEASONED FLOUR WITH SALT, OR BETTER YET MSG, PEPPER, PAPRIKA, AND CAYENNE)
- 4 C PANKO BREADCRUMBS
- 4 6-OZ VEAL OR CHICKEN CUTLETS, POUNDED TO ¼-INCH THICK
- ¼–½ C VEGETABLE OIL

OPTIONAL SIDE DISH AND GARNISHES

- YOUR FAVORITE POTATO SALAD
- CHOPPED CHIVES
- CHOPPED PARSLEY
- FRIED CAPERS

INSTRUCTIONS

Prepare salad

1. Preheat oven to 400 degrees. Prepare fennel by cutting off the stalks, trimming the bottom, and quartering the bulb from top to bottom. Cut the core, but leave enough to keep fennel held together. Toss fennel with olive oil and sprinkle with salt and pepper. Roast in oven for 15 minutes or until fennel is softened and lightly browned. Cool and dice. This should yield about 2 cups.

2. Prepare pickled onions by heating apple cider vinegar and sugar in a small saucepan until sugar dissolves. Pour vinegar solution over sliced onion, covering completely, and let pickle for 30 minutes–1 hour. Drain.

3. In a large bowl, toss together fennel, onions, tomatoes, parsley, capers, and smoked trout.

CONTINUES ON NEXT PAGE

— PERLY'S RESTAURANT AND DELICATESSEN —

PRESERVED LEMON VINAIGRETTE

1 preserved lemon rind, minced	3 Tbsp white sugar	½ c mild olive oil
1 Tbsp smooth Dijon mustard	3 Tbsp white wine vinegar	Salt and pepper, to taste

In a small food processor or blender, blend lemon rind, mustard, sugar, and vinegar.

Slowly add olive oil to the food processor while it is running. The mixture should thicken and emulsify.

Add salt and pepper to taste and thin with water, if needed, to reach desired consistency.

Cook veal schnitzel

1. Scramble 4 eggs with about 1 tablespoon of water (no milk is added to keep the dish kosher), and place in a shallow dish. Place seasoned flour and panko into individual shallow dishes.

2. Dredge pounded veal or chicken in seasoned flour, dip in egg wash, and press into panko breadcrumbs.

3. Heat a large, heavy-bottomed skillet with vegetable oil over medium-high heat. There should be enough oil to generously coat bottom of pan.

4. Fry breaded cutlets for about 2 minutes per side, until golden brown. Hold in a warm oven (250–300 degrees) until ready to plate. (Note: Alternatively, you can spray each piece of veal with pan spray and bake in a 400-degree oven until browned on both sides. This makes less of a mess, but does not give you the same crispiness you get from frying.)

Cook sunny side up eggs

1. Oil bottom of a nonstick skillet and heat over medium heat. Crack 2 eggs into pan and cook until egg whites are set.

2. Cook remaining eggs in pairs and set aside. Do not worry about them being hot; warm to room temperature is fine.

Assemble

1. Dress salad with vinaigrette and toss.

2. At the restaurant, we put a small scoop of homemade dill potato salad in the center of the plate. Any quality potato salad will suffice. This acts as an anchor for the veal and keeps it from sliding, but is optional.

3. Place fried veal cutlet atop potato salad.

4. Place sunny side up eggs on top of veal.

5. Place fennel and parsley salad atop eggs.

6. Finally, "Essen! Essen!"

— PERLY'S RESTAURANT AND DELICATESSEN —

ALMOND HORNS

From pastry chef Chelle Bravo, this gluten-free confection gets a triple dose of almonds with almond paste, almond meal, and sliced almonds. Add a little dark chocolate to the equation and you have a perfect horseshoe-shaped cookie.

YIELD: 20 COOKIES

Ingredients

- 3 C ALMOND PASTE
- 1½ C SUGAR
- 3 TSP ALMOND EXTRACT
- ¾ C ALMOND MEAL OR FINELY GROUND ALMONDS
- 2 LARGE EGG WHITES, ROOM TEMPERATURE
- 2 C SLICED ALMONDS
- 1 C BITTERSWEET CHOCOLATE, CHOPPED

INSTRUCTIONS

1. In a large bowl, mix almond paste and sugar until well blended.

2. Add almond extract, almond meal, and egg whites. Mix until fully blended and smooth.

3. Portion dough into 2-ounce pieces and roll into balls.

4. Roll each ball in sliced almonds, then roll into 4-inch logs. Gently bend into U-shaped cookies.

5. Transfer horns to a parchment-lined cookie sheet and let dry, uncovered, for at least 30 minutes.

6. Preheat oven to 350 degrees. Bake for 16 minutes.

7. While cookies are cooling, melt chocolate in a double boiler or microwave. Dip ends of cooled cookies into melted chocolate and place on a parchment-lined plate. Place in refrigerator until chocolate has set.

CHAPTER
FOUR

5 CHEFS

13 RECIPES

TASTES *from* ABROAD

If your palate has wanderlust, we've got you covered. These internationally seasoned chefs have ventured abroad and brought their favorite flavors back home for the rest of us to enjoy, recreating their journeys in our backyard. Combining the best local ingredients with their newly discovered techniques, this group of chefs has reinvented classics and created their own.

The kitchens at Deco Ristorante and Graffiato Richmond send out dishes night after night that would make Sicilian grandmothers proud. Saison's Adam Hall and Jay Bayer traveled to Central and Latin America and, lucky for us, they've never really left. And Metzger's Brittanny Anderson and the rest of her sausage-centric team became enthralled with the flavors and updated favorites of German cooking. Now no one in this town can figure out how we went this long without it.

As opposed to the last chapter where we embraced Richmond's distinct personalities from within, these four restaurants have done a stunning job bringing outside influences into our community. And they've done so in a way that's most distinctly Richmond.

— CHAPTER FOUR: TASTES FROM ABROAD —

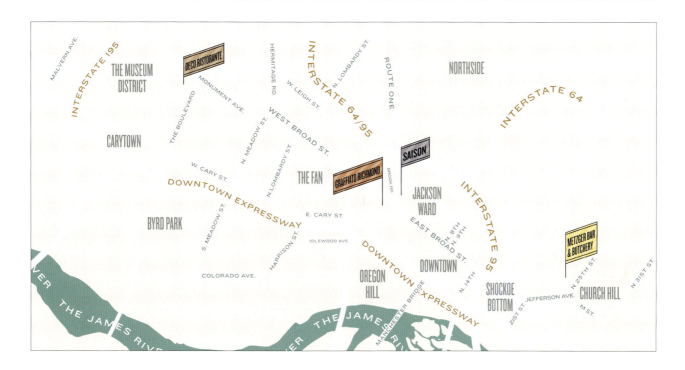

GRAFFIATO RICHMOND

MIKE ISABELLA & MATT ROBINETT

Burrata with Tomato, Corn, Arugula, and Country Bread

Bucatini Carbonara

Baller Status

A Maymont Afternoon

METZGER BAR & BUTCHERY

BRITTANNY ANDERSON

Smoked Trout Rillettes

Beer-Brined Pork Chops

Spätzle

Brown Sugar Bay Leaf Ice Cream

DECO RISTORANTE

GIUSEPPE SCAFIDI

Insalata di Finocchi

Pasta Trinacria

SAISON

ADAM HALL

Rundown

Chorizo Pâté

Peruvian Roast Chicken

MENU

BURRATA WITH TOMATO, CORN, ARUGULA, AND COUNTRY BREAD

BUCATINI CARBONARA

BALLER STATUS

A MAYMONT AFTERNOON

GRAFFIATO RICHMOND

CHEFS
MIKE ISABELLA AND MATT ROBINETT

Richmond was all aflutter when news broke that celebrity chef Mike Isabella would be opening a second Graffiato location in our fair city. As list after list touted Richmond's under-the-radar foodie status, the arrival of Graffiato seemed to suggest the city's reputation wasn't so hidden.

In many ways, Graffiato Richmond mirrors its sister restaurant in D.C. When looking for a space, Mike wanted to keep the same industrial feel, with brick walls, wood floors, and high, exposed ceilings. He found it in the former Popkin Tavern. "When I walked in," he says, "I thought, 'this is it.'"

And some of his signature dishes carried over, of course. The pepperoni sauce that earned so much praise on *Top Chef All-Stars* is present, served with a barbecued chicken thigh, shaved fennel, and sorrel. The Jersey Shore pizza, topped with fried calamari, also made the trip down I-95.

But Mike didn't just pluck Graffiato D.C. and drop it two hours south.

Some dishes, like the burrata salad—which Mike says works well with local Billy Bread and seasonal vegetables from local farms—were developed specifically for the local market, often in partnership with Graffiato Richmond's chef de cuisine Matt Robinett.

Matt got his start at a small seafood restaurant in Gloucester, Va., before working for the Williamsburg Inn, the Ryland Inn in Whitehouse Station, N.J., and other well-regarded restaurants up and down the East Coast. He was looking for a way to come back home when the opportunity to work with Mike arose.

"When I took the position, they had just finished gutting the building," Matt says. "We still had to decide what the menu was going to be. Mike and I sat down one afternoon and wrote the whole menu."

Mike and Matt continue to work together to develop new menu items, but local products often serve as a starting point. "It's easy to look at a farmer's list and pick out ideas," Matt says. "We've got a whole section of the menu that's dedicated to nothing but vegetables, which is great."

According to Mike, it's more than just vegetables. "There are a lot of great farms, great breweries, and distilleries," he says.

"You have everything you need in Virginia. You don't have to go elsewhere. It was the perfect match for our style of food."

Those close ties with farmers are just one example of how Mike and Matt are working to make sure Graffiato isn't just a flashy name, but a part of Richmond's food culture.

"It's been a great experience working with the chefs and the culinary team in Richmond," Mike says. "I've done a lot of events out there. I've done events with the chefs coming up to my restaurants in D.C. Some came in for our pre-opening to give us feedback. We really just work together and believe in each other. I think that's a big part of becoming part of a community out there."

— GRAFFIATO RICHMOND —

photo by Greg Powers

WHAT'S YOUR FAVORITE DISH TO COOK FOR FAMILY AND FRIENDS?

Mike: I do love a nice caciopepe. It's spaghetti or bucatini, a noodle like that. And then it's water, Parmesan cheese, pepper, and butter.

Matt: Braised short ribs. I always do it with either stone-ground grits or polenta. It's one of the most comforting things and I love braising and slow cooking. It's one of my favorite things to do. It's always a winning meal.

WHAT'S THE STRANGEST INGREDIENT YOU'VE EVER WORKED WITH?

Mike: Cod sperm. It had a really weird smell. It's like eggs. It's creamy and it's in a sack. I fried it and served it with some citrus.

Matt: Duck testicles. I confited them and then sautéed them.

WHERE DO YOU GO OUT TO EAT?

Mike: Purple Pig in Chicago, Bestia in L.A., Thip Khao in D.C. I eat all over the country. I don't have a lot of favorite restaurants; I just go to a lot of restaurants.

Matt: I crave everything Peter Chang cooks. Those damn scallion pancakes are so good. My son's three years old and he knows Peter Chang's by name.

WHAT'S YOUR FAVORITE KITCHEN MUSIC?

Mike: I have open kitchens in all my restaurants so we don't play music because we're basically in the dining room. At home, I do like a little bit of hip-hop. I enjoy having it upbeat to keep me going.

Matt: Late-'80s punk. Minor Threat's one of my favorites, and the Ramones.

WHAT'S THE LAST MEAL YOU MADE FOR YOURSELF?

Mike: Yesterday, me and my wife, we made a pasta salad with a lot of vegetables, and peppers with some nice Italian sausage. I'm Italian, I eat simple.

Matt: Marinated grilled flank steak and a bunch of grilled vegetables.

— GRAFFIATO RICHMOND —

"THERE ARE A LOT OF GREAT FARMS, GREAT BREWERIES, AND DISTILLERIES. YOU HAVE EVERYTHING YOU NEED IN VIRGINIA. YOU DON'T HAVE TO GO ELSEWHERE. IT WAS THE PERFECT MATCH FOR OUR STYLE OF FOOD."
—MIKE ISABELLA

"IT'S EASY TO LOOK AT A FARMER'S LIST AND PICK OUT IDEAS. WE'VE GOT A WHOLE SECTION OF THE MENU THAT'S DEDICATED TO NOTHING BUT VEGETABLES."
—MATT ROBINETT

— GRAFFIATO RICHMOND —

BURRATA WITH TOMATO, CORN, ARUGULA, AND COUNTRY BREAD

YIELD: 6 SERVINGS

This is a great dish to eat when the tomatoes and corn are at their peak in the height of summer. At Graffiato, we cold smoke the burrata, which is a nice contrast to the refreshing and herbaceous tomato and corn salad. If you can't find burrata, a high-quality mozzarella will definitely suffice.

INGREDIENTS

- 2 EARS SWEET CORN, HUSK INTACT
- 2 OZ EXTRA VIRGIN OLIVE OIL
- 6 SLICES COUNTRY-STYLE BREAD, SLICED ¾-INCH THICK
- 6 BURRATA
- ½ LB SMALL HEIRLOOM TOMATOES, MEDIUM DICED
- ½ RED ONION, FINELY DICED
- 2 CLOVES GARLIC, MINCED
- 3 OZ RED WINE VINAIGRETTE (RECIPE ADJACENT)
- 8 LARGE BASIL LEAVES
- 8 MINT LEAVES
- KOSHER SALT, TO TASTE
- FRESHLY GROUND BLACK PEPPER, TO TASTE
- 2 OZ ARUGULA
- MALDON OR FLEUR DE SEL SEA SALT, TO TASTE

INSTRUCTIONS

1. Place corn in a preheated 400-degree oven or over a hot grill and roast until husks are charred and kernels are sweet and tender, 10–12 minutes.
2. Allow to cool, then shuck corn, making sure to remove all silk. Cut the kernels off the cob and set aside.
3. Brush olive oil on bread and either grill or toast until golden brown. Cut the bread slices in half and place on a large platter, leaving space in the middle for the tomato salad.
4. Cut each burrata in half and place one half on each piece of bread.
5. In a large bowl, mix together the corn, tomato, red onion, garlic, and red wine vinaigrette. Tear basil and mint into little pieces and add to the tomato mixture. Season with kosher salt and pepper and place in the middle of the platter.
6. Garnish with arugula leaves, a drizzle of olive oil, and a sprinkle of sea salt. Serve immediately.

RED WINE VINAIGRETTE

- ¼ c red wine vinegar
- ¾ c canola or grapeseed oil
- ½ tsp shallot, minced
- ¼ tsp garlic, minced
- ½ tsp salt

Whisk all ingredients together and shake vigorously before use.

— GRAFFIATO RICHMOND —

BUCATINI CARBONARA

YIELD: 6 SERVINGS

This dish is an adaptation of an Italian classic. At Graffiato, we extrude our own semolina bucatini pasta, which you can do at home with the help of a pasta press for a KitchenAid® stand mixer. It's well worth the time and effort. Otherwise, we recommend a high-quality dried pasta, such as Rustichella d'Abrusso.

CONTINUES ON NEXT PAGE

— GRAFFIATO RICHMOND —

— GRAFFIATO RICHMOND —

Ingredients

- 6 TBSP ENGLISH PEAS
- 2 TBSP EXTRA VIRGIN OLIVE OIL + 2 TBSP TO TOP PASTA
- ¼ LB GUANCIALE OR BACON, DICED
- 1 SHALLOT, MINCED
- 4 CLOVES GARLIC, MINCED
- 2 OZ WHITE WINE
- 3 C HEAVY WHIPPING CREAM
- 2 OZ PARMESAN, FINELY GRATED + 2 OZ TO TOP PASTA
- 3 TBSP FRESH LEMON JUICE
- 2 TBSP WHITE DISTILLED VINEGAR
- 1¼ LB BUCATINI
- 6 LARGE EGGS
- 3 TBSP CHIVES, CHOPPED
- KOSHER SALT, TO TASTE
- FRESHLY GROUND BLACK PEPPER, TO TASTE
- MALDON SEA SALT, TO TASTE

INSTRUCTIONS

1. Blanch peas: Bring a pot of heavily salted water to a rapid boil. Prepare an ice bath to shock peas and stop the cooking. Plunge peas into boiling water and cook until just tender, approximately 1 minute. Immediately plunge cooked peas into the ice bath. Strain peas and reserve.

2. Heat 2 tablespoons of olive oil in large sauté pan over medium heat and add guanciale or bacon. Reduce heat to medium low and render until crispy, 7–10 minutes. Strain meat, reserving 1 tablespoon of fat in the pan.

3. Add shallot and garlic to the pan and sweat over low heat until soft and translucent.

4. Deglaze pan with white wine and bring to a simmer. Reduce liquid until thick and syrupy, and the pan is almost dry.

5. Add cream, bring to a boil, and reduce to a simmer. Simmer until reduced to approximately 1½ cups. Whisk in 2 ounces of Parmesan and the lemon juice. Set aside.

6. In the meantime, prepare a large pot of heavily salted water and bring to a rapid boil for the pasta. Also, prepare a small pot of salted water with the vinegar and bring to a fast simmer for the eggs.

7. Drop pasta in water and cook until al dente, about 7 minutes for dried or about 5 minutes for fresh.

8. Once pasta is almost done, poach eggs. Drop eggs, one at a time, into the pot with the vinegar and cook until egg whites are set but the yolk is still viscous, about 3 minutes. Remove the eggs onto a towel with a slotted spoon and season with a bit of salt and pepper.

9. Place the cream mixture back on the stove and bring to a boil. Add in the reserved guanciale or bacon and the peas.

10. Strain the pasta, reserving some of the pasta water, and add the pasta to the cream sauce with about an ounce of the reserved pasta water. Add chives and a healthy amount of ground black pepper. Taste and adjust seasoning with salt, pepper, or lemon juice if needed. If the sauce is too thick, add a little more pasta water; the sauce should just coat the pasta.

11. Place pasta into 6 bowls and top each with a soft poached egg. Drizzle with remaining olive oil and top with the remaining Parmesan. Serve immediately, allowing your guests to break the egg into the pasta.

— GRAFFIATO RICHMOND —

BALLER STATUS

YIELD: 1 COCKTAIL

Ingredients

1½ OZ MONKEY SHOULDER SCOTCH

1 OZ LUXARDO AMARETTO

½ OZ FRESH LEMON JUICE

HOUSEMADE GINGER BEER

5 DASHES ANGOSTURA BITTERS

CANDIED GINGER

INSTRUCTIONS

Combine scotch, amaretto, and lemon juice in a shaker tin with ice. Shake vigorously and strain into a collins glass. Top with ice and ginger beer. Add 5 generous dashes of Angostura bitters. Garnish with candied ginger.

A MAYMONT AFTERNOON

YIELD: 1 COCKTAIL

INGREDIENTS

1 EGG WHITE

1½ OZ BELLE ISLE PREMIUM MOONSHINE

¾ OZ LAVENDER SIMPLE SYRUP

¾ OZ CARPANO BIANCO VERMOUTH

½ OZ FRESH LEMON JUICE

FRESH LAVENDER BUD

INSTRUCTIONS

Carefully separate egg white into a shaker tin, then add moonshine, simple syrup, vermouth, and lemon juice. Seal tin and give it a good dry shake without ice. Once nicely frothed, add ice and wet shake until tin is cold. Strain into a chilled coupe. Garnish with a fresh lavender bud.

METZGER
BAR & BUTCHERY

With owners who come from Sausage Craft, Belmont Butchery, the Relay Foods meat department, and a restaurant housed on a working farm, it's no surprise that meat is given prime billing at Metzger Bar & Butchery.

In fact, the restaurant began with Brad Hemp and Nathan Conway considering a retail space for Sausage Craft. When Brittanny Anderson moved back home to Richmond after training and working as a chef in New York City, she took a job at the artisan sausage company while she made plans to open her own restaurant. That's where the three joined forces and Metzger began to take shape.

Brittanny Anderson

"At first it was just butchery and meat themed," Brittanny says. "Then we talked with our designer and he came up with the name Metzger and we became a German restaurant."

While the crew knew their way around a butchery, German cooking was new territory. Sitting at the bar—which was crafted from an oak tree from actor Robert Duvall's Fauquier County farm—Brittanny flips through the stack of well-worn German cookbooks she frequently consults. The books are covered in Post-it notes with ideas for fresh takes on the traditional recipes. "I'll take these weird recipes and ingredients and think about how we could make it cooler, about ways to make it more modern and interesting."

The menu at Metzger features a lot of pork and speck, as well as housemade cheeses like ricotta and crème fraîche, which Brittanny describes as "very German farm wife." German standards like schnitzel and spätzle were menu must-haves.

Dishes also embody a complex layering of flavors and textures. "I'm a firm believer in like with like," Brittanny says. "If I've got radishes in a dish, I'm going to have radishes on there a couple of ways, like a braised radish, a raw radish, a pickled radish, all on one plate. I also think a lot about textures. I want to have a crunchy, a pickley, a salty, a sweet, and a chewy. I always think about the layers of dishes."

What you won't find at Metzger are waiters dressed in lederhosen and accordion players serenading customers. "We wanted it to stand out as a space that isn't kitschy," Brittanny says. "We talked a lot about Berlin when we were designing the space; it's such a cool, modern, arty city."

"We wanted the vibe to be casual, but with a really high level of service and quality of food. I want people to be able to eat here on a Thursday night because they don't have anything at home, but also when they have a special birthday. You can get something really fancy, or you can sit at the bar and have schnitzel and a beer."

RECIPES

SMOKED TROUT RILLETTES

BEER-BRINED PORK CHOPS

SPÄTZLE

BROWN SUGAR BAY LEAF ICE CREAM

— METZGER BAR & BUTCHERY —

"I'LL TAKE THESE WEIRD RECIPES AND INGREDIENTS AND THINK ABOUT HOW WE COULD MAKE IT COOLER, ABOUT WAYS TO MAKE IT MORE MODERN AND INTERESTING."
—BRITTANNY ANDERSON

WHAT'S YOUR FAVORITE DISH TO COOK FOR FAMILY AND FRIENDS?

Cassoulet. A big pot of beans, meat, and sausage—I mean, you can't go wrong. It lasts for like a week in your house.

WHAT ARE YOUR GO-TO INGREDIENTS?

Celery. We pickle celery. We do celery minionette. We braise celery. I love celery. It's an underutilized vegetable.

WHERE DO YOU GO OUT TO EAT?

Peter Chang's, Saison, Pho Tay Do, The Dog and Pig Show.

WHAT'S THE LAST MEAL YOU MADE FOR YOURSELF?

Probably chilaquiles. I like to make breakfast nachos. We eat more breakfast that I cook for myself. At dinnertime we just eat cheese and meat and wine.

WHAT'S YOUR FAVORITE KITCHEN MUSIC?

Beyonce, and we've been listening to a lot of Backstreet Boys lately. Oh my gosh, so embarrassing. Heart's number one. Circle that.

WHAT'S THE STRANGEST INGREDIENT YOU'VE EVER WORKED WITH?

Probably when I was on *Chopped*, and I had to use ridiculous things like gummy tarantulas and Pop Rocks.

WHAT WAS YOUR INTRODUCTION TO COOKING?

I cooked at Patina in the West End for Brian Mumford. It was my first cooking job, my first time in a professional kitchen. It was a great experience—big place, lots of dudes. Taught me to be tough.

— METZGER BAR & BUTCHERY —

SMOKED TROUT RILLETTES

YIELD: ABOUT 2 CUPS

Rillettes is rustic version of pâté and is usually make with minced pork. Brittanny Anderson keeps it fresh by using smoked trout, lemon, and parsley. These rillettes are delicious spread on crackers and even better with a glass of crisp Grüner Veltliner.

INGREDIENTS

- ⅓ C LEEKS, SLICED THINLY CROSSWISE
- ½ + 2½ TBSP BUTTER, SOFTENED
- 1 SMALL SPRIG THYME
- ⅛ C WHITE WINE, LIKE GRÜNER VELTLINER
- 8 OZ SMOKED TROUT, SKINNED AND PICKED OF BONES
- 4 OZ MASCARPONE OR CREAM CHEESE, SOFTENED
- ⅛ C CRÈME FRAÎCHE
- 2 TSP + 2 TBSP PARSLEY, CHOPPED
- 1 TBSP FRESH LEMON JUICE
- ¼ TSP LEMON ZEST
- SALT AND PEPPER, TO TASTE

INSTRUCTIONS

1. Sauté leeks in ½ tablespoon butter over low heat without getting any color on the vegetable, about 5 minutes.
2. Once soft, add thyme and deglaze the pan with white wine. Simmer and reduce liquid by half, then remove from heat.
3. Remove thyme and pour leek mixture into a mixer fitted with a paddle attachment.
4. Add trout, mascarpone, crème fraîche, parsley, lemon juice and zest, and remaining butter and mix on low speed until combined and uniform. Season with salt and pepper to taste. Serve with toast and garnish with fresh parsley.

— METZGER BAR & BUTCHERY —

— METZGER BAR & BUTCHERY —

BEER-BRINED PORK CHOPS

YIELD: 4 SERVINGS

Brining adds salt to the meat and helps retain moisture. The flavor is at its best, and the process is well worth the extra effort. Nothing is better than a thick cut of brined pork that is perfectly grilled—except for a side of homemade spätzle, of course.

Ingredients

- ½ C COARSE KOSHER SALT
- ⅓ C SUGAR
- 2 BAY LEAVES
- 10 PEPPERCORNS
- ½ SMALL ONION, SLICED
- ½ LEMON, SLICED
- 5 CLOVES GARLIC, SMASHED
- 6 C WATER
- 4 C BEER
- 4 BONE-IN, CENTER CUT PORK CHOPS, 1- TO 1½-INCH THICK (ABOUT 1 LB EACH)
- ½ C DEMI-GLACE
- SALT AND PEPPER, TO TASTE

CONTINUES ON NEXT PAGE

SPÄTZLE

YIELD: 4 SERVINGS

Often the simplest dishes are the best, and spätzle is no exception. This incredibly easy recipe is best served sautéed with a little butter and herbs.

INGREDIENTS

- 2 C ALL-PURPOSE FLOUR
- 1 TSP SALT
- 4 EGGS, BEATEN
- ¼ C MILK
- 2 TBSP BUTTER
- 2 TBSP CHOPPED FRESH HERBS OF YOUR CHOICE (PARSLEY, BASIL, TARRAGON)
- SALT AND PEPPER, TO TASTE

CONTINUES ON PAGE 143

— METZGER BAR & BUTCHERY —

IN THE KITCHEN WITH BRITTANNY ANDERSON | BEER-BRINED PORK CHOPS

INSTRUCTIONS

1. Make brine: Combine first 8 ingredients in a medium pot and bring to a boil. Once salt and sugar have dissolved, turn off heat and let steep for 30 minutes. Pour beer into the brine and chill until cold.

2. Pour cold brine over pork chops and brine for 2 hours in the refrigerator.

3. Remove pork from brine, pat dry, and season with salt and pepper. On a hot grill or skillet, cook pork for about 5 minutes per side or until chops are a medium doneness (internal temperature of about 150 degrees). At the restaurant, we serve the pork with spätzle (recipe pg. 141), about 2 Tbsp of demi-glace per serving, and a simple green salad.

— METZGER BAR & BUTCHERY —

IN THE KITCHEN WITH BRITTANNY ANDERSON | SPÄTZLE

INSTRUCTIONS

1. In large bowl, mix together flour and salt. Make a well in the center of the flour and add eggs and milk. Slowly whisk to incorporate the wet and dry ingredients and beat until lumps are gone. The dough will be thinner than cookie dough but thicker than cake batter.

2. Meanwhile, heat a pot of salted water to boiling and place a large colander or perforated hotel pan over the top of the pot. Prepare a large bowl of ice water to chill the spätzle as they come out of the pot.

3. Working in batches, pour about a cup of batter into the colander or perforated pan and scrape it through holes using a bench scraper or spatula. Once all dough been forced through, remove the colander. When spätzle has floated to the top of the boiling water, remove it with a slotted spoon and place in ice water. Continue until all spätzle has been cooked.

4. To serve, drain the spätzle and sauté with butter and chopped herbs. Season with salt and pepper to taste.

— METZGER BAR & BUTCHERY —

BROWN SUGAR BAY LEAF ICE CREAM

YIELD: 8 SERVINGS

Few things are as satisfying as making homemade ice cream. Bay leaves add a bit of sophistication to the ultra-rich custard base. It's the secret ingredient that will keep everyone guessing why your ice cream is so good.

INGREDIENTS

- 1½ C WHOLE MILK
- 1½ C HEAVY CREAM
- 1 VANILLA BEAN
- 10 BAY LEAVES
- 1 C BROWN SUGAR
- 10 EGG YOLKS
- PINCH OF SALT

INSTRUCTIONS

1. Add milk and cream to medium saucepan.
2. With a sharp paring knife, split vanilla bean in half lengthwise and scrape out beans with the blade of the knife. Add both vanilla beans and pod to the pot with milk mixture.
3. Add bay leaves to pot and bring to a simmer over medium heat.
4. Once simmering, remove from the heat and cover. Let steep for at least 15 minutes or up to 1 hour.
5. Meanwhile, whisk brown sugar, egg yolks, and salt until pale and fluffy.
6. Slowly pour hot milk mixture into bowl with eggs yolks while whisking to ensure the eggs do not curdle.
7. Pour mixture back into the pot and cook over low heat until thickened, 3–5 minutes.
8. Strain mixture through a fine mesh strainer into a bowl set over ice. Remove bay leaves, vanilla pod, and any lumps.
9. Once completely chilled, process according to ice cream maker specifications.
10. Freeze for at least 1 hour until ice cream is firm.

CHEF

GIUSEPPE
SCAFIDI

MENU

INSALATA
DI
FINOCCHI

PASTA
TRINACRIA

DECO RISTORANTE

The island of Sicily is a confluence of cultures. As Greeks, Romans, Arabs, Spaniards, French, and countless others invaded, they left behind their languages, architecture, and cuisine. As the centuries passed, these historic influences merged and morphed, creating a culture that no longer belonged to these occupiers, but could only be claimed by Sicily itself.

One could say that Giuseppe Scafidi and Deco Ristorante represent a similar melding of influences.

Giuseppe grew up helping his grandmother in the kitchen, snapping peas and cooking eggplant. "I was right next to her every time she was cooking," he says. "I really learned how to cook in a simple way with my hands." She taught him traditional Sicilian recipes that emphasize simplicity and let fresh ingredients shine.

From there, he went on to work in an Italian coffee shop and a trendy restaurant housed in a 13th-century building adorned with frescoes and Arab architectural details. That's when he began to develop an appreciation for architecture and food—and the relationship between the two.

"The two really go side by side," he says. "For me, there is no food without architecture, there is no architecture without food."

Giuseppe eventually landed in Richmond and wanted to share his love of food, architecture, and Sicily. He helped open Azzurro Restaurant and Stuzzi before his first solo foray with Deco Ristorante.

"At Deco, I got to make my own decisions about the food, about the business, about the architecture, about the sign—about every detail," he says. "I always like to do the creative and the architectural details in every place I go. It's the pleasure and the satisfaction of doing something creative."

He started with an art deco gas station in Devil's Triangle.

"There were a few elements of architecture that I wanted to recover in this building and make something beautiful, and save it," he says. "I wanted to bring life back to the art deco in the neighborhood."

Inside, he serves up his grandmother's traditional Sicilian recipes as well as modern and American takes on classic dishes. Some, like the insalata di finocchi and pasta trinacria, are seen on these pages. Others hold too much emotional connection to his grandmother to ever reveal them.

"It's not just the way my grandmother taught me to cook," he says. "It's from my house in Sicily. It's what I cook in my house now, what I cook for my kids. It's tradition. I wanted to introduce that to everyone."

— DECO RISTORANTE —

"It's not just the way my grandmother taught me to cook. It's from my house in Sicily. It's what I cook in my house now, what I cook for my kids. It's tradition. I wanted to introduce that to everyone."

—Giuseppe Scafidi

WHAT'S THE STRANGEST INGREDIENT YOU'VE EVER WORKED WITH?

Spleen. It's really traditional from Sicily. We use everything from the animal, and with the spleen, we make a sandwich. It's fantastic. It's unusual for American people, but one day I'm going to do it and see how people like it.

WHAT'S YOUR FAVORITE KITCHEN MUSIC?

Music is too distracting for me. It takes me away when I am cooking. Out front is different. I like jazz out front.

WHAT'S THE LAST MEAL YOU MADE FOR YOURSELF?

We had a wine dinner yesterday, so my last meal was octopus carpaccio and fresh pasta with sauce. It was beautiful.

— DECO RISTORANTE —

— DECO RISTORANTE —

— DECO RISTORANTE —

INSALATA DI FINOCCHI

YIELD: 2 SERVINGS

Fennel and orange is a classic flavor combination that is only made better with olives, pomegranate seeds, and mint. This simple and fresh salad is a gorgeous addition to any classic Italian meal, with its pops of orange, crimson, and green.

INGREDIENTS

- 1 HEAD FENNEL
- SEGMENTS OF 1 ORANGE
- 1 TBSP POMEGRANATE SEEDS
- 5 LARGE GREEN OLIVES, PITTED AND CHOPPED
- 6 FRESH MINT LEAVES + 4 LEAVES
- JUICE OF 1 ORANGE
- JUICE OF 1 LEMON
- 1 TBSP EXTRA VIRGIN OLIVE OIL
- SALT AND PEPPER, TO TASTE

INSTRUCTIONS

1. Cut stalks from the top of the fennel and discard. Then trim the bottom of the bulb and remove the outer layer and discard.

2. Thinly slice the bulb to about ⅛-inch thick with a mandolin, starting with the side of the bulb. If you don't have a mandolin, thinly slice with a very sharp knife.

3. In a large bowl, add fennel, orange segments, pomegranate seeds, olives, and mint leaves.

4. In a medium bowl, whisk together orange juice, lemon juice, olive oil, salt, and pepper to taste.

5. Pour dressing over fennel mixture and toss.

6. Transfer salad to a serving plate and garnish with mint leaves. Serve immediately.

— DECO RISTORANTE —

PASTA TRINACRIA

YIELD: 2 SERVINGS

Don't let the simplicity of this dish fool you. It's layered with flavor, from roasted peppers and meaty eggplant to briny capers and olives and a hint of spice from the red pepper flakes. But despite everything that goes into the sauce, there is just enough to coat the pasta, which is the star.

Ingredients

- 4 TBSP GRAPESEED OIL, OR ANY NEUTRAL OIL
- 3½ C EGGPLANT, PEELED AND MEDIUM DICED
- 1 RED PEPPER
- 1 YELLOW PEPPER
- 2 TBSP EXTRA VIRGIN OLIVE OIL
- 1 TSP GARLIC, MINCED
- 1 TBSP CAPERS
- 8 SICILIAN BLACK OLIVES
- 1 C STORE-BOUGHT MARINARA SAUCE
- 1 PINCH CRUSHED RED PEPPER FLAKES
- SALT, TO TASTE
- 4 OZ DRIED BUSIATE PASTA OR YOUR FAVORITE LONG PASTA
- 8 BASIL LEAVES + 2 LEAVES
- 2 OZ RICOTTA SALATA, SHAVED

INSTRUCTIONS

1. In a large skillet, heat grapeseed oil over medium-high heat. Sauté eggplant until golden, 10–15 minutes. At first the oil will completely absorb into the eggplant, but as it cooks, the oil will release. Drain eggplant on paper towels and set aside.

2. Roast peppers on a grill or over a gas burner flame, turning regularly. Once the skin is blackened, remove skin and seeds. Cut into long, thin strips and set aside.

3. In a large skillet, heat olive oil over medium heat. Sauté garlic, capers, olives, and peppers until garlic is a golden color, 2–4 minutes.

4. Add marinara, cooked eggplant, and red pepper flakes to the pan and cook for about 2 minutes. Season with salt to taste, but keep in mind the olives and capers are salty. Remove from heat.

5. Bring a large pot of salted water to a boil and cook pasta according to the package instructions. Add cooked pasta to skillet with sauce and add 8 basil leaves. Cook pasta and sauce over medium-high heat for about 1 minute.

6. Portion pasta onto two plates and garnish with a basil leaf and shaved ricotta salata.

— DECO RISTORANTE —

SAISON

As a child, Saison chef Adam Hall would sit at the counter, do his homework, and watch his mom at work in the kitchen. One day, she asked him to join her and started to teach him to make a few basic dishes.

Cooking with his mom turned into a series of jobs in restaurant kitchens, reading stacks of cookbooks, and experimenting at home.

"I got more serious about cooking," he says. "I'd just read cookbooks and challenge myself on my own. I'd use that as a testing ground for anything I thought was interesting."

While working at Capital Ale House, he met Jay Bayer. The two shared a passion for food and homebrewing and it wasn't long before they started tossing around ideas for opening their own restaurant.

They spent a year negotiating on a space in Jackson Ward, sometimes walking away and considering other buildings and neighborhoods. But they always came back.

"We wanted to be a neighborhood restaurant," Adam says. "There wasn't really anything like that in Jackson Ward."

"In two years, it's changed dramatically. When we moved in, the building across the street was boarded up, another was condemned. Now they're all rented out and there are all these other restaurants in the neighborhood. It's just really cool—there's this exploding scene in this micro-pocket of Richmond."

Much of the menu at Saison is inspired by Adam and Jay's wanderlust spirit. The two travel frequently, especially in Central and Latin America. "I like off-the-beaten-path traveling," Adam says. "The colors, the food—it's a whole different side of life than in America."

Everything from street food to fine dining infuses Adam's dishes, like the chorizo pâté or the Rundown—a seasonal seafood dish served with sweet potato and coconut-habanero broth.

"Small plates can be a little weird and I get to experiment with hot ingredients and fun things," Adam says. "But we have a whole spectrum of dishes for the everyday eater. We've got to play the line to find neutrality for everyone."

Whether it's their travel-inspired food, selection of craft beer, or seasonal cocktail menu, Adam says they just want Saison to represent the people behind the bar and in the kitchen. "These are things we all nerd out about and want to show people."

CHEF

ADAM HALL

MENU

RUNDOWN

CHORIZO PÂTÉ

PERUVIAN ROAST CHICKEN

— SAISON —

WHAT ARE YOUR GO-TO INGREDIENTS?

Garlic, chilis, butter, stock. Stock is the blood of our kitchen. We make our stock out of pigs' feet. It's used in almost every single thing.

WHERE DO YOU GO OUT TO EAT?

Joe's Inn.

WHAT'S THE LAST MEAL YOU MADE FOR YOURSELF?

Chili cheese hot dogs.

WHAT'S YOUR FAVORITE DISH TO COOK FOR FAMILY AND FRIENDS?

Fried chicken.

WHAT'S YOUR FAVORITE KITCHEN MUSIC?

During dinner service I don't like any music. During prep I like something light, like Django Reinhardt or something kind of easy.

"I like off-the-beaten-path traveling. The colors, the food—it's a whole different side of life than in America."

—ADAM HALL

— SAISON —

RUNDOWN
SEAFOOD, SWEET POTATO, COCONUT-HABANERO BROTH

— SAISON —

YIELD: ABOUT 7 SERVINGS

This Southeast Asian-inspired dish is made with the freshest seafood at the market. Once the coconut milk-based broth is prepared, the dish comes together in a matter of minutes; it's cooked just long enough for the seafood to cook through.

INGREDIENTS

- 1¾ C SWEET POTATOES, COOKED AND DICED
- 1 LB BABY OCTOPUS
- 1 LB SEA SCALLOPS, CUT IN HALF
- 1 LB LARGE SHRIMP
- 2 LBS MUSSELS
- 5 GREEN ONIONS, THINLY SLICED ON A BIAS
- 7 C COCONUT-HABANERO BROTH (RECIPE ADJACENT)
- 2 FRESNO CHILI PEPPERS, OR ANY SPICY RED PEPPER, THINLY SLICED
- 2 TBSP MICRO CILANTRO
- 1 LIME, CUT INTO WEDGES (OPTIONAL)
- 2 RADISHES, THINLY SLICED

INSTRUCTIONS

1. In a large saucepan, add first seven ingredients.
2. Bring to a boil over high heat and cook until mussels have opened, about 5 minutes.
3. Divide evenly into serving bowls and garnish with sliced peppers, micro cilantro, lime, and sliced radish.

COCONUT-HABANERO BROTH

- 1 Tbsp vegetable oil
- ½ white onion, chopped
- ½ carrot, peeled and chopped
- ½-inch piece fresh ginger, peeled and chopped
- 5 cloves garlic, crushed
- 5 sprigs thyme
- ¼ tsp ground allspice
- ¼ tsp turmeric
- ½ tsp chipotle powder
- ½ c clam juice
- 1 habanero, chopped
- 56 oz (4 cans) unsweetened coconut milk
- Salt, to taste

In a large saucepan, heat vegetable oil over medium heat. Add onion, carrot, ginger, and garlic. Cook until onions are translucent and soft, but do not let brown.

Add thyme, allspice, turmeric, and chipotle powder. Stir and cook for about 30 seconds.

Add clam juice and bring to a simmer. Cook until liquid has reduced by half.

Add habanero and coconut milk and simmer for 45 minutes.

Strain through a chinois or fine mesh strainer. Add salt to taste.

— SAISON —

IN THE KITCHEN WITH ADAM HALL | RUNDOWN

— SAISON —

― SAISON ―

CHORIZO PÂTÉ

YIELD: 12–16 SERVINGS

This pâté is made with classic French technique but Adam Hall infuses a healthy dose of Southwestern flavors. Pickles wonderfully complement the richness of this highly spiced meat. Try it with pickled red onion, jalapeño, and mustard seed.

Ingredients

- 2¼ LBS BONELESS PORK BUTT, TRIMMED OF EXCESS FAT
- ½ TBSP CUMIN SEEDS
- ½ TBSP BLACK PEPPERCORNS
- ½ TBSP CAYENNE PEPPER
- ½ TBSP CHIPOTLE
- 4½ OZ PORK LIVER, CLEANED OF SINEW (CHICKEN LIVER MAY BE SUBSTITUTED IF NECESSARY)
- ½ C CILANTRO, CHOPPED
- 3 CLOVES GARLIC, FINELY CHOPPED
- 2¼ TBSP KOSHER SALT
- 2¼ TBSP ALL-PURPOSE FLOUR
- 2 EGGS, BEATEN
- 1½ TBSP TEQUILA BLANCO
- 2 TBSP MICRO CILANTRO

INSTRUCTIONS

1. Cut pork butt into 1-inch chunks.
2. Toast cumin seeds and black peppercorns in a dry skillet over medium-low heat. Stir continuously and toast until spices are fragrant, 2–3 minutes. Transfer to a spice grinder and grind fine.
3. In a large bowl, mix together pork, spices, liver, cilantro, and garlic. Freeze until ingredients just start to freeze on the surface, 1–2 hours.
4. Pass meat mixture through a grinder fitted with a small die over a chilled bowl. Be sure grinder equipment is very cold.
5. Add salt, flour, eggs, and tequila to ground pork and mix thoroughly. This is your forcemeat.
6. Preheat oven to 325 degrees.
7. Put forcemeat into a terrine and knock it on the table a few times to remove any air bubbles. Cover tightly with foil.
8. Place terrine into a hotel or roasting pan and pour in warm water until it is two-thirds up the terrine mold.
9. Bake until internal temperature reaches 160 degrees, 2 hours–2 hours 15 minutes.
10. Remove terrine from oven and let cool to room temperature. Cover surface with plastic wrap or parchment paper. Place a hard flat surface (such as another terrine pan or cardboard) on top. Weight the top of the terrine with several heavy cans and refrigerate overnight.
11. To serve, run a sharp knife along the sides of the pan and unmold. Slice and serve with micro cilantro garnish.

— SAISON —

PERUVIAN ROAST CHICKEN

— SAISON —

YIELD: 2–4 SERVINGS

Adam pulled out all the stops to make this chicken the best it can be. Not only is a whole chicken brined and marinated, but it's also spatchcocked, a method of removing the spine and flattening the chicken so it roasts evenly at high temperatures.

INGREDIENTS

- 1 WHOLE CHICKEN, 4–5 LBS
- 1 GALLON WATER
- ¾ C KOSHER SALT
- ½ C DARK BROWN SUGAR
- 2–4 TBSP PERUVIAN MARINADE (RECIPE ADJACENT)
- 1 RED CHILI PEPPER, THINLY SLICED
- 1 TBSP MICRO CILANTRO

INSTRUCTIONS

1. Trim chicken of excess fat, but leave the neck fat because it helps retain the marinade.

2. Carefully loosen skin from breast and thighs, without detaching the skin from the chicken. This ensures the brine will have direct contact with the meat.

3. In a large pot, bring water, salt, and brown sugar to a boil. Stir until salt and sugar dissolve. Completely cool the brine and add the chicken, making sure it is completely submerged. Brine in refrigerator for 8–12 hours.

4. Remove chicken from the brine and pat dry.

5. Spatchcock the chicken: In this preparation method, the chicken's spine is removed. Using very sharp kitchen spears, cut along both sides of the spine and remove it from the bird (you can reserve the spine to make stock). Place chicken breast-side up so it lays flat. With even pressure, push down hard on the chicken shoulders to expose the breastbone and flatten the chicken.

6. Using your fingers, work around the breastbone and pull the whole bone out, including the cartilage that runs to the bottom of where the breast meets.

7. Next remove the wishbone, which is easily found by feeling the neck area. Make small incisions just under each side and, using your fingers, remove the wishbone.

8. Using a spoon, gently spread Peruvian marinade under the skin, being careful not to rip the skin. Move the marinade around to make as much contact with the meat as possible, squeezing it down to the legs.

9. Let chicken rest for 1 hour at room temperature in preparation to roast.

10. Preheat oven to 425 degrees.

11. Place a cooling rack over a parchment-lined sheet tray. Lay chicken over the rack, breast-side up, and roast until the thickest part of the chicken reaches 165 degrees and its juices run clear, 35–45 minutes.

12. Remove from oven and let rest for 10–15 minutes. Carve chicken into serving pieces and garnish with a few slices of red chili pepper and micro cilantro. Serve with roasted fingerling potatoes.

PERUVIAN MARINADE

- ½ c fresh mint, chopped
- 2 tsp jalapeño, chopped
- 12 cloves garlic, chopped
- 6 Tbsp olive oil
- 4 Tbsp salt
- 2 Tbsp black pepper
- 2 Tbsp cumin powder
- 2 Tbsp sugar
- 4 tsp smoked paprika
- 4 tsp Mexican oregano
- 4 tsp lime zest
- ½ c lime juice

Add all ingredients to a food processor and puree until uniform.

CHAPTER FIVE
OUT OF THE ORDINARY

5 CHEFS

12 RECIPES

We decided to round out this second collection of Richmond's finest on a bit of an unconventional note.

Every once in a while, a restaurant can take your preconceived notions and knock them on their can. A suburban tavern or a back alley bar may be dishing out insanely intricate food and beverage pairings. A new venture between two award-winning chefs may actually appeal to the whole family—including your "food critic" aunt. And a French restaurant may turn out to be anything but pretentious or serious.

A few of the following chefs aren't new to 804ork either—we know them, and we know their work. However, they continue to push their flavors and surprise us with new concepts, new offerings, and new menu items that we can't wait to get our hands on.

— CHAPTER FIVE: OUT OF THE ORDINARY —

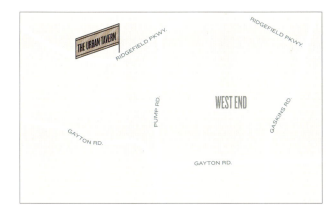

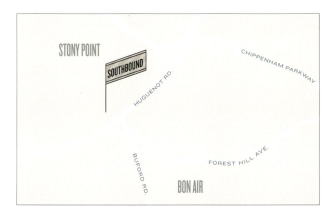

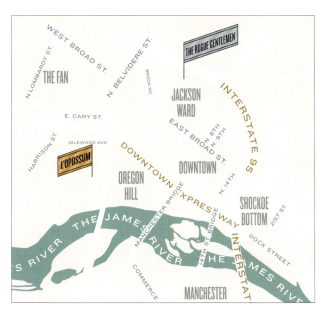

SOUTHBOUND

JOE SPARATTA & LEE GREGORY

Pastrami-Cured Salmon

Cauliflower Soup

Fresh Pasta with Braised Short Ribs

THE URBAN TAVERN

TIM BEREIKA

Salmon Tartare, Avocado, Coriander, and Preserved Lemon

Roasted Cauliflower, Brown Butter, Capers, and Pistachio Gremolata

Risotto-Style Farro with Asparagus, Oyster Mushrooms, and Parmesan

THE ROGUE GENTLEMEN

JOHN MAHER

Duck Confit with Fava Beans, Artichokes, Morels, Fennel, and Carrot-Chèvre Puree

Pickled Mackerel, Beets, Sorrel, Miso and Beet Vinaigrette, Pistachio, and Mint

Dolores Park

L'OPOSSUM

DAVID SHANNON

Sweetbreads with Lobster and Grits

Foie Gras with Strawberry and Rhubarb

Hot Black Bottom à la Mode

SOUTHBOUND

 JOE SPARATTA AND LEE GREGORY

 PASTRAMI-CURED SALMON | **CAULIFLOWER SOUP** | **FRESH PASTA WITH BRAISED SHORT RIBS**

As any Richmonder knows, the neighborhoods that pepper the city have their own identities. For a restaurant to become a true neighborhood destination, it has to tap into the tastes and personalities of those who live right down the street.

That's why, when Joe Sparatta and Lee Gregory set out to open a joint restaurant in Southside, they knew they couldn't just recreate Heritage and The Roosevelt—they had to create a place that fit. And as residents of Bon Air, the two also knew just what their neighborhood needed.

"We were always hearing, 'I wish there was somewhere to eat out here,'" Joe says.

"There are a couple good places, for sure, but it seems to be dominated by chains. For people who have families and are limited on time and don't necessarily want to come to the city all the time, there are very few options for them."

So what does that mean at Southbound? Simple, casual, and family-friendly. A nice place for people to eat and drink without being too fancy.

In short, the neighborhood gathering place.

For two chefs with their own restaurants and approaches to cooking, Joe and Lee found the collaborative effort to be an easy transition.

"We already had the same thought process when it comes to food," Joe says. "We think in similar manners. We had a singular vision. We wanted to create something new that was a combination between all of us."

Their shared focus on simplicity doesn't mean Southsiders are still stuck crossing the river for more adventurous fare (although Joe says they do see Southbound as an opportunity to introduce new clientele to Heritage and The Roosevelt).

At Southbound, you'll find fried chicken sandwiches and bacon double cheeseburgers served alongside fusilli pasta with short ribs and scallops with celery puree and confit tomato. Kids aren't consigned to chicken nuggets, either. Instead, they can choose from elevated standbys like chicken breast with local grits or mac and cheese made with house-made elbows and four cheeses.

"We're trying to have something for everyone," Lee said in *Style Weekly*. "We want to be an everyday restaurant. This restaurant is very much location-specific. I don't think we would have done this—we weren't just going to open a restaurant together. It never would have happened downtown or in the Fan or Church Hill. It's Southside-specific."

— SOUTHBOUND —

"WE ALREADY HAD THE SAME THOUGHT PROCESS WHEN IT COMES TO FOOD. WE THINK IN SIMILAR MANNERS. WE HAD A SINGULAR VISION. WE WANTED TO CREATE SOMETHING NEW THAT WAS A COMBINATION BETWEEN ALL OF US."

—JOE SPARATTA

WHAT'S YOUR FAVORITE DISH TO COOK FOR FAMILY AND FRIENDS?

Joe: I really like doing fish collars a lot. It's a great way for the table to actually interact with each other. It forces people to get weird and be uncomfortable about the anatomy of that collar. It's bone-in and you are learning about these new morsels of awesome fish that normally don't get eaten.

WHAT ARE YOUR GO-TO INGREDIENTS?

Joe: I've been using a lot of pepper mash lately. It's the byproduct of us making hot sauce. After we make and puree the hot sauce, we strain it off, dehydrate the leftover mash, and then powder it. It's this acidic, really bright, spicy, awesome little condiment.

WHERE DO YOU GO OUT TO EAT?

Joe: Curry Craft, The Roosevelt, The Magpie, Full Kee, Metzger Bar & Butchery.

WHAT'S THE STRANGEST INGREDIENT YOU'VE EVER WORKED WITH?

Joe: Durian. It's a southeast Asian custard fruit. It's this really large spiny fruit. It smells like a rotting deer carcass. I'm not kidding. But it tastes incredible.

WHAT'S THE LAST MEAL YOU MADE FOR YOURSELF?

Joe: We actually did short rib cheesesteaks, just took a little piece of short rib scrap and turned it into a delicious cheesesteak. I like more garbage comfort food than cooking a nice composed meal for myself.

— SOUTHBOUND —

— SOUTHBOUND —

PASTRAMI-CURED SALMON WITH SLOW-COOKED EGG, PICKLED MUSTARD SEED, AND RYE "CRUNCH"

PICKLED MUSTARD SEEDS

- 1 c apple cider vinegar
- 2 Tbsp brown sugar
- ½ c water
- 1 tsp salt
- ½ c mustard seeds

Combine everything but mustard seeds in a saucepan and bring to a slow simmer.

Add mustard seeds and cook until all liquid is absorbed, about 10 minutes.

YIELD: 10 SERVINGS

This dish has a lot of components, but each is easy to prepare. You can prep everything the day before, and leisurely compose an appetizer that is almost too pretty to eat.

INGREDIENTS

- 1½ C SALT
- ¾ C SUGAR
- 3 TBSP GROUND BLACK PEPPER
- 2 TBSP ONION POWDER
- 2 TSP GARLIC POWDER
- 1 TSP FRESH GARLIC, MINCED
- 2 BUNCHES FRESH CILANTRO, CHOPPED
- 1 BUNCH FRESH FLAT LEAF PARSLEY, CHOPPED
- 2 BAY LEAVES, CHOPPED
- 1 SIDE FRESH SALMON, BONES REMOVED AND SKINNED
- ½ C SORGHUM
- 2 TBSP CAYENNE PEPPER
- 2 TBSP PAPRIKA
- 2 TBSP GROUND CORIANDER
- 1 TBSP WHITE VINEGAR
- 10 EGGS
- 2 SLICES RYE BREAD (WE USE RYE FROM SUB ROSA BAKERY)
- SALT AND PEPPER, TO TASTE
- 1¼ C CRÈME FRAÎCHE
- 5 TBSP DILL, CHOPPED
- ½ C PICKLED MUSTARD SEEDS (RECIPE ADJACENT)
- ⅓ C MICRO HERBS
- ⅓ C SALMON ROE
- 2 RADISHES, VERY THINLY SLICED

CONTINUES ON NEXT PAGE

INSTRUCTIONS

PREPARE PASTRAMI-CURED SALMON

1. In a large bowl, mix together the first 9 ingredients.

2. Coat both sides of salmon with herb and salt mixture, packing on any extra rub.

3. Place salmon on a wire rack over a sheet tray, and refrigerate for 2–3 days. The salmon should feel dry.

4. Scrape the rub from the fish and pat dry.

5. In a saucepan over medium-high heat, combine sorghum, cayenne, paprika, and coriander and boil for 1 minute.

6. After the glaze has cooled to warm, brush salmon on both sides and refrigerate overnight.

7. Cut salmon on a bias as thin as possible.

COOK 6-MINUTE EGGS

1. Prepare an ice water bath to shock eggs when they are finished cooking.

2. Add white vinegar to a saucepan of water and bring to rolling water.

3. Gently add cold eggs at the peak of boil, and set a timer for 6 minutes.

4. After 6 minutes, submerge eggs in ice water for 5 minutes. Peel and set aside.

— SOUTHBOUND —

IN THE KITCHEN WITH LEE GREGORY & JOE SPARATTA | PASTRAMI-CURED SALMON WITH SLOW-COOKED EGG, PICKLED MUSTARD SEED, AND RYE "CRUNCH"

PREPARE RYE "CRUNCH"

1. Toast rye bread until quite dry and browned, but not burnt.

2. Cut the rye into small pieces and grind in a spice grinder with salt and pepper to taste. Set aside.

PREPARE DILL CRÈME FRAÎCHE

» Mix together crème fraîche and dill. Set aside.

ASSEMBLE

1. Smear about 2 Tbsp of dill crème fraîche on each plate.

2. Artfully place 6 or 7 slices of salmon over dill crème fraîche.

3. Dot each slice with a little pickled mustard seed and sprinkle with micro herbs.

4. Place a small spoonful of rye "crunch" and salmon roe in between the salmon slices.

5. Top the dish with a few slice of radish and serve each plate with 1 egg.

— SOUTHBOUND —

CAULIFLOWER SOUP

YIELD: 2–4 SERVINGS

This soup is easy enough to make on a weeknight, yet elegant enough to impress dinner party guests. The chutney with almonds, raisins, and curry adds an unexpected element that makes this soup memorable.

ALMOND CHUTNEY

- 3 Tbsp sherry vinegar
- 1 Tbsp brown sugar
- ½ tsp salt
- ½ c sliced almonds
- ¼ c golden raisins
- 1 Tbsp Indian Madras curry powder
- Water

In a medium saucepan, add sherry vinegar, brown sugar, and salt. Cook until sugar and salt are dissolved.

Add remaining ingredients and enough water to cover almonds and raisins. Slowly simmer all ingredients until remaining liquid has a syrup-like consistency.

Ingredients

- 2 HEADS CAULIFLOWER
- 2 TBSP OLIVE OIL
- 1 SMALL ONION, CHOPPED
- 2 CLOVES GARLIC, MINCED
- 1 BAY LEAF
- 1 QT CHICKEN STOCK
- 1 QT HALF-AND-HALF
- SALT AND FRESHLY GROUND BLACK PEPPER, TO TASTE
- ALMOND CHUTNEY (RECIPE BELOW)
- 4–5 TBSP EXTRA VIRGIN OLIVE OIL

INSTRUCTIONS

1. Remove leaves and thick core from cauliflower and chop coarsely.

2. Heat olive oil in a large saucepan or soup pot over medium heat and add the onion and garlic. Cook until softened, but not browned, about 5 minutes.

3. Add cauliflower, bay leaf, chicken stock, and half-and-half and bring to a boil. Reduce heat to a simmer, cover, and cook until cauliflower is very soft and falling apart, about 15 minutes. Remove from heat.

4. Remove bay leaf. Using a handheld immersion blender, puree the soup. Alternatively, puree in small batches in a blender and return to the pot. Season with salt and black pepper to taste. Garnish with almond chutney and a drizzle of olive oil.

— SOUTHBOUND —

— SOUTHBOUND —

FRESH PASTA WITH BRAISED SHORT RIBS

YIELD: 6 SERVINGS

Braising is like magic. It takes the most humble cuts of meat and makes them succulent and tender—not that short ribs need a lot of help. With a little assistance from some aromatics, this sauce showcases the essence of this fantastic cut of beef.

INGREDIENTS

- 3 LBS SHORT RIBS
- 1 TBSP SEA SALT
- 1 TBSP BLACK PEPPER
- 2 TBSP + 2 TBSP VEGETABLE OIL
- 1 ONION, DICED
- 1 LARGE CARROT, PEELED AND DICED
- 3 STALKS CELERY, DICED
- 3 CLOVES GARLIC, MINCED
- 4 BAY LEAVES
- 1½ QT CHICKEN STOCK
- 2 TBSP WHOLE-GRAIN MUSTARD
- 1 C SOUR CREAM
- 2 TBSP CHIVES, CHOPPED
- SALT AND PEPPER, TO TASTE
- 30 OZ FRESH PASTA
- 6 TBSP CRÈME FRAÎCHE
- 4 TBSP CHIVES, CHOPPED
- 3 TBSP RICOTTA SALATA, FRESHLY GRATED
- 2 TBSP MICRO HERBS

INSTRUCTIONS

1. Preheat oven to 350 degrees.
2. Pat short ribs dry with a paper towel and season with salt and pepper.
3. Heat 2 tablespoons vegetable oil in a large skillet over medium-high heat. Sear short ribs on all sides and set aside.
4. In a large pot, add remaining 2 tablespoons vegetable oil and place over medium heat. Add onion, carrot, celery, and garlic and cook until onions are translucent, 6–8 minutes. Be sure not to brown the vegetables.
5. Add browned short ribs and bay leaves to the pot and cover with chicken stock.
6. Remove pot from heat and cover with plastic wrap and foil. Place in oven to braise for 2 hours.
7. Remove short ribs from liquid and pull meat into shreds. Set aside.
8. Place the pot with the braising liquid back on the stove over medium-high heat and reduce liquid to nappe (when it coasts the back of a spoon), 8–10 minutes. Remove from heat.
9. Stir in whole-grain mustard, sour cream, pulled short ribs, and chives. Season with salt and pepper to taste. Keep warm while pasta cooks.
10. Bring a large pot of salted water to a boil and cook fresh pasta for 1–3 minutes. Drain and serve with braised short ribs.
11. In a small bowl, mix together crème fraîche and chopped chives. Garnish each plate with about 1 tablespoon chive crème fraîche, grated ricotta salata, and micro herbs.

THE URBAN TAVERN

Tim Bereika

When we last left Tim Bereika, he was crafting Mediterranean-inspired small plates to pair with the well-curated wine selection at Secco Wine Bar.

He's since exchanged bottles of wine for taps of beer, but at The Urban Tavern, the complementary nature of food and drink still takes the spotlight.

"The fundamentals are the same," Tim says. "There are flavors and nuances that come out of wine and beer. You just think about complementary flavors that go with them."

The Urban Tavern's beer-centric concept is the brainchild of Garland Taylor, owner of Home Team Grill, and John Csukor of culinary consulting agency KOR Food Innovation. As they were building the restaurant

and the brand, they realized a chef was needed to carry the creative process beyond the opening and develop seasonally driven menus. That's when Tim came on board.

While some may see a concept restaurant and think only of the limitations, Tim says The Urban Tavern is actually the opposite. "I have a lot of creative freedom with the menu," he says. "My background is more regional Italian cuisine, so being a part of this concept is really cool and refreshing because I'm encouraged to use other worldly flavors as well. It's fun for me because it's not something that I have done a lot in the past."

Tim's creative process often begins with seasonal ingredients. Sometimes that means building a recipe around a vegetable with a short season, like asparagus. At other times, he takes "seasonless" ingredients and prepares them in ways that reflect what diners seek out at different times of year, such as the roasted cauliflower with brown butter, capers and pistachio gremolata.

His process is also a collaborative one. He frequently bounces ideas off his sous chef, Jeff Collins, as well as Garland and the team at KOR.

"We taste through, we discuss some concerns and questions, we talk out loud," he says. "Through a period of a few adjustments, a new menu is born."

"It's a collaborative thing and it will always be that way. It's not just one person that makes this successful. It's the team, the whole group of people that are involved."

Tim recently started combining his artist background with his passion for food through video filming and editing. At timbereika.com, he demonstrates cooking techniques and recipes, including the dishes featured here.

MENU

SALMON TARTARE, AVOCADO, CORIANDER, AND PRESERVED LEMON VINAIGRETTE

ROASTED CAULIFLOWER, BROWN BUTTER, CAPERS, AND PISTACHIO GREMOLATA

RISOTTO-STYLE FARRO WITH ASPARAGUS, OYSTER MUSHROOMS, AND PARMESAN

— THE URBAN TAVERN —

"IT'S A COLLABORATIVE THING AND IT WILL ALWAYS BE THAT WAY. IT'S NOT JUST ONE PERSON THAT MAKES THIS SUCCESSFUL. IT'S THE TEAM, THE WHOLE GROUP OF PEOPLE THAT ARE INVOLVED."

—TIM BEREIKA

WHAT ARE YOUR GO-TO INGREDIENTS?

At the restaurant: Aleppo pepper, olive oil, fresh herbs, curry. At home: Pasta.

WHAT'S YOUR FAVORITE DISH TO COOK FOR FAMILY AND FRIENDS?

I make a lot of fresh pasta, in any way, shape, or form. Pasta is so versatile. In colder months, you bake it; warmer months, you just dress it lightly.

WHAT'S THE STRANGEST INGREDIENT YOU'VE EVER WORKED WITH?

When I was in Italy, I had to prepare a dish with two things that were really strange. One was basically cow breast. It was strange; it was like a paste. Then the reproductive organ was basically the fallopian tube and the ovary. In most places in Europe, they use everything. And I mean everything.

WHAT'S YOUR FAVORITE KITCHEN MUSIC?

My favorite band is Fu Manchu. But I have been listening to old country music lately, like Waylon Jennings, Johnny Cash, and Hank Williams, stuff like that.

WHAT WAS YOUR INTRODUCTION TO COOKING?

My grandfather was probably one of Julia Child's biggest admirers. When we came down to visit, he would always be in the kitchen all day cooking and we would always have pretty elaborate dinners. I think that was my first experience with good food.

— THE URBAN TAVERN —

SALMON TARTARE, AVOCADO, CORIANDER, AND PRESERVED LEMON VINAIGRETTE

YIELD: 2 SMALL PLATES

Salmon tartare is a rich, yet refreshing, dish. Raw salmon has a clean flavor and unctuous texture that is complemented by avocado, a classic accompaniment. Preserved lemons add just the right amount of salt and acid to lift the palate.

INGREDIENTS

- 9 OZ GOOD QUALITY, VERY FRESH SALMON
- 2 TBSP PRESERVED LEMON VINAIGRETTE (RECIPE PG. 183)
- SALT, TO TASTE
- ½ C AVOCADO PUREE (RECIPE PG. 183)
- 2 TBSP CILANTRO LEAVES
- 1 TBSP PRESERVED LEMON RIND, CUT INTO SLIVERS

INSTRUCTIONS

1. Chop salmon into pieces the size of corn kernels. Then toss with preserved lemon vinaigrette. Season with salt to taste.

2. Smear avocado puree around the sides of two bowls. Divide fish evenly between both bowls and garnish with fresh cilantro and preserved lemon rind.

— THE URBAN TAVERN —

AVOCADO PUREE

- 1 ripe avocado, skin and pit removed
- 1½ tsp red onion, finely chopped
- 1 clove garlic, minced
- 1 lime, juice and zest
- ¼ tsp ground cumin seed
- ¼ tsp ground coriander seed
- ¼ tsp fresh cilantro, chopped
- ½ tsp kosher salt
- 1 Tbsp extra virgin olive oil

Combine all ingredients and puree until smooth. Reserve in refrigerator in an airtight container.

PRESERVED LEMON VINAIGRETTE

- 2 Tbsp preserved lemon, minced
- 3 Tbsp lemon juice
- 1 Tbsp honey
- 1 tsp fresh thyme, chopped
- ½ c extra virgin olive oil
- Kosher salt and pepper, to taste

Add first four ingredients to a food processor and blitz. With the processor running, slowly drizzle in the olive oil. Season dressing with kosher salt and freshly ground black pepper to taste. Store in refrigerator in an airtight container.

— THE URBAN TAVERN —

ROASTED CAULIFLOWER, BROWN BUTTER, CAPERS, AND PISTACHIO GREMOLATA

YIELD: 2 SMALL ENTRÉES

While The Urban Tavern focuses on seasonal ingredients, cauliflower is available year-round. It's the preparation—in this case, a pistachio gremolata—that brings a fresh quality to the seasonless vegetable.

INGREDIENTS

- ⅓ C FLAT LEAF PARSLEY, FINELY CHOPPED
- ⅓ C UNSALTED PISTACHIOS, FINELY CHOPPED
- 1 CLOVE GARLIC, MINCED
- ZEST OF 1 LEMON
- FINELY GROUND SEA SALT, TO TASTE
- GROUND ALEPPO PEPPER, TO TASTE
- ¼ C UNSALTED BUTTER
- ½ HEAD CAULIFLOWER, FLORETS ONLY
- 1 TBSP CAPERS, RINSED AND DRAINED

INSTRUCTIONS

1. Make pistachio gremolata: Combine first six ingredients in a bowl. Place in a sealed container and reserve in refrigerator.

2. Preheat oven to 425 degrees.

3. Melt butter in a medium saucepan over medium-high heat. Once melted and hot, add cauliflower and stir so florets are coated in butter. Continue to cook over medium-high heat until cauliflower begins to caramelize and butter starts to brown a little.

4. Transfer cauliflower to a baking sheet and roast in the oven until florets are cooked through and have browned more, 7–8 minutes.

5. Remove roasted cauliflower from oven and season lightly with salt. Place cauliflower into an appropriately sized bowl, pour over any remaining brown butter from the pan, and top with reserved pistachio gremolata and capers.

— THE URBAN TAVERN —

RISOTTO-STYLE FARRO WITH ASPARAGUS, OYSTER MUSHROOMS, AND PARMESAN

YIELD: 2 SERVINGS

Farro hails from Italy and is an ancient wheat with a pleasant nutty flavor. When it's slowly cooked with the gradual addition of stock, it takes on a slightly creamy quality similar to risotto.

Ingredients

- 1 TSP + 2 TBSP EXTRA VIRGIN OLIVE OIL
- 3 OZ OYSTER MUSHROOMS, CLEANED AND CUT INTO BITE-SIZED PIECES
- 2 TBSP YELLOW ONION, FINELY CHOPPED
- 1 CLOVE GARLIC, MINCED
- 6½ OZ SEMI-PEARLED FARRO
- 3 TBSP WHITE WINE
- 3 C CHICKEN STOCK, HEATED
- 2 OZ (ABOUT 4 SPEARS) ASPARAGUS, SLICED ON A BIAS ABOUT ⅛-INCH THICK
- ¼ C + 1 TBSP GRATED PARMESAN
- 1 TBSP UNSALTED BUTTER
- KOSHER SALT, TO TASTE
- MICRO BASIL

INSTRUCTIONS

1. Heat 1 teaspoon of olive oil in a skillet over medium-high heat and sauté oyster mushrooms until they have released their liquid and have browned slightly. Reserve at room temperature.

2. Place a fresh saucepan over medium heat and add remaining 2 tablespoons of olive oil. Once oil is hot, add onion and cook until translucent, 2–3 minutes.

3. Add garlic and farro to the pan and continue to cook for a few minutes.

4. Pour in wine and stir until evaporated, then add 1 cup of hot chicken stock. Reduce heat to medium low and continue to stir farro until stock is absorbed. Repeat the process with remaining 2 cups of stock. Farro is ready when grains are soft on the outside, slightly al dente in the middle, and there's a little bit of creamy liquid left in the pan.

5. Once all stock is incorporated, add asparagus and sautéed mushrooms.

6. Remove farro from heat and vigorously stir in ¼ cup Parmesan and butter.

7. Season farro with kosher salt to taste. Divide it evenly into two bowls, top with remaining Parmesan and micro basil, and serve.

RECIPES

DUCK CONFIT WITH FAVA BEANS, ARTICHOKES, MORELS, FENNEL, AND CARROT-CHÈVRE PUREE

PICKLED MACKEREL, BEETS, SORREL, MISO AND BEET VINAIGRETTE, PISTACHIO, AND MINT

DOLORES PARK

THE ROGUE GENTLEMEN

CHEF JOHN MAHER

John Maher has spent the last 18 years traveling, moving around, and cooking. After college at Johnson and Wales in Rhode Island, he worked at restaurants in New York City, Germany, Napa, and the Caribbean. But it was during his time in San Francisco that John found something he wanted to bring back to his hometown of Richmond.

"I'd go to these bars and they had a very specific feel," he says. "I love the pre-Prohibition era, the golden age of bartending. I wanted to bring that feel of a world-class cocktail bar back to Richmond."

John looked at several spaces in Church Hill, but never found anything with the right vibe. Then a friend called about a building he had recently purchased in Jackson Ward.

There were no floors or walls, but John says he walked in the door and could immediately picture where everything would go.

"I knew I wanted to have the bar be the focus, right when you walk in," he says. "It's all old heart pine from 1908 from an old tobacco warehouse. I think it just frames what we're doing really well."

Bartenders masterfully serve up a seasonal selection of classic cocktails like the Dolores Park, a blend of gin, pineapple and lemon juices, and housemade falernum, topped with a splash of IPA beer. Or opt for the dealer's choice—just choose a flavor pairing like floral and refreshing, weird and herbal, or spicy and boozy and trust your bartender to take it from there.

"I approach our drink menu from a culinary perspective," John says. "We use more savory ingredients. I've never been a bartender [until opening The Rogue Gentlemen]. I think differently from career bartenders."

The same attention to detail found in the glass is also present on the plate. John worked to develop a menu of modern American small plates and entrées, such as duck confit with fava beans, roasted artichokes, morels, fennel, and carrot-chèvre puree.

John sees the combination of simple, ingredient-driven food and handcrafted cocktails as his contribution to a food scene he watched develop and thrive while traveling all those years—one he's happily joining now.

"No matter how far away I get, Richmond sucks me back every time," he says. "There was no cocktail bar and I saw a hole to fill. I felt like I had a good shot at making something special."

— THE ROGUE GENTLEMEN —

"I'd go to these bars and they had a very specific feel. I love the pre-Prohibition era, the golden age of bartending. I wanted to bring that feel of a world-class cocktail bar back to Richmond."

—John Maher

WHAT WAS YOUR INTRODUCTION TO COOKING?

Martin Yan and his TV show *Yan Can Cook*. When I was a kid, I would get off the school bus and go watch him on TV. I think I was like 8 years old, and I asked for a cleaver for my birthday. My parents, of course, didn't think that a cleaver belonged in an 8-year-old's hands, so they gave me a wok instead. Outside of cooking with my mom and things like that, that was my first holy shit moment.

WHAT ARE YOUR GO-TO INGREDIENTS?

Rye whiskey.

WHAT'S THE STRANGEST INGREDIENT YOU'VE EVER WORKED WITH?

Cod sperm.

WHAT'S YOUR FAVORITE DISH TO COOK FOR FAMILY AND FRIENDS?

I've always enjoyed a really well-done roast chicken. It's hard to do it right. I like keeping it simple when I cook at home.

WHERE DO YOU GO OUT TO EAT?

Shoryuken Ramen, Saison.

WHAT'S THE LAST MEAL YOU MADE FOR YOURSELF?

It was like 3 in the morning and I made steak and eggs.

WHAT'S YOUR FAVORITE KITCHEN MUSIC?

For prepping, I jam out to Whitney Houston. And I'm not ashamed at all to say it.

— THE ROGUE GENTLEMEN —

DUCK CONFIT
WITH FAVA BEANS, ARTICHOKES, MORELS, FENNEL, AND CARROT-CHÈVRE PUREE

YIELD: 2 SERVINGS

Confit is a menu buzzword that is actually an old French technique for preservation. Duck is submerged in its own rendered fat and cooked low and slow all day. This results in ultra-tender meat that falls off the bone with the slightest touch of a fork.

INGREDIENTS

- 2 PEKING DUCK HINDQUARTERS AND BREASTS
- 4 C RENDERED DUCK FAT, MELTED
- ¼ C + ¼ C KOSHER SALT
- ½ C FAVA BEANS, PODS REMOVED

- 2 ARTICHOKES
- JUICE OF 2 LEMONS
- 1 MEDIUM CARROT, PEELED AND CUT INTO 1-INCH SEGMENTS
- 1 TSP + 2 TSP + 1 TBSP VEGETABLE OIL

- 4 OZ CHÈVRE
- 1 C VEGETABLE STOCK
- 1 BULB FENNEL, MEDIUM DICED
- 1 TSP SHALLOT, FINELY DICED

- 6 MOREL MUSHROOMS
- 1 TSP GRAPESEED OIL
- 1 BUNCH THYME, CHOPPED
- SALT AND PEPPER, TO TASTE

FOR DUCK CURE:
- ¼ C KOSHER SALT
- 1 TBSP BROWN SUGAR
- 1 BAY LEAF
- 1 TBSP THYME, CHOPPED

- ¼ BUNCH FLAT LEAF PARSLEY
- ⅓ TSP BLACK PEPPER

CONTINUES ON NEXT PAGE

INSTRUCTIONS

Confit the duck

1. Mix all duck cure ingredients in a mortar and pestle and grind together until well blended. Thoroughly rub cure on both sides of duck, making sure they are completely coated. The best ratio is 2 tablespoons of rub to every pound of duck. Cover duck and let sit in refrigerator for 24 hours.

2. Rinse duck of all excess salt and pat dry with a towel. Place duck in a baking dish that is deep enough to submerge duck in fat.

3. Preheat oven to 190 degrees.

4. Pour melted duck fat over the duck until covered. Cover with aluminum foil and place in the center of the oven. Bake for about 8 hours, or until falling-off-the-bone tender.

5. Remove from oven and allow the duck to cool in the fat. Once cool, place in refrigerator to rest overnight.

Blanch fava beans

1. Bring 1 quart of water and ¼ cup kosher salt to a boil.

2. Add fava beans and blanch for 1 minute.

3. Strain beans and shock in ice water.

4. Once cooled, remove skins by pinching the surface and tearing away. Set aside.

Cook artichokes

1. Clean artichokes by using a pairing knife and peeler to remove the exterior petals. Next, cut out the fibrous tissue at the base.

2. Cut artichoke hearts into quarters, and place in 1 quart of water with the juice of one lemon. This prevents oxidization.

3. Bring another quart of water to a boil with juice of 1 lemon and ¼ cup salt. Add artichokes and place a small plate or bowl over them to keep them submerged. Cook until artichokes are easily pierced with a pairing knife. Remove and set aside

Prepare carrot-chèvre puree

1. Preheat oven to 350 degrees.

2. Coat carrots with 1 teaspoon vegetable oil and season with salt and pepper to taste. At the same time, prepare and roast the fennel (see steps below).

3. Roast until tender, about 30 minutes.

4. Add carrots and chèvre to a blender with a splash of vegetable stock. Blend, while slowly adding more stock, until the puree is loose enough to coat a spoon and is the consistency of thick soup. Set aside.

Prepare fennel and mushrooms

1. Toss diced fennel with 2 teaspoons vegetable oil and season with salt and pepper to taste.

2. Place on a parchment-lined baking sheet and roast at 350 degrees until tender and lightly caramelized, 25–30 minutes.

3. Add 1 tablespoon vegetable oil to a sauté pan over medium-low heat. Add diced shallots and toss in oil. Add morels and sauté for 1–2 minutes. Be careful not to overcook shallots and morels. They have a delicate flavor that can be damaged from too much heat.

Cook duck confit

1. Remove duck legs from rendered fat and use your hands to scrape off any excess fat.

2. Twist the protruding bone gently so it will release from the meat but not tear the meat apart. Pull the bones out and discard.

3. Heat another sauté pan over medium heat and add grapeseed oil. Place the duck in the pan, skin-side down, and brown until crisp. Be careful to not burn the skin.

4. Place duck in a 350-degree oven to warm it through, 5–8 minutes.

5. Remove from oven and cut duck into 1-inch cubes. Be sure to keep the skin intact, as it is very important for flavor and texture.

Assemble

1. To plate, take a spoon and spread carrot-chèvre puree across 2 plates.

2. Artfully arrange the vegetables across the top of the puree.

3. Place duck confit pieces in the same manner over the vegetables.

4. Garnish with fresh chopped thyme and serve.

PICKLED MACKEREL, BEETS, SORREL, MISO AND BEET VINAIGRETTE, PISTACHIO, AND MINT

YIELD: 2 SERVINGS

If you are looking for a unique salad, this beautifully composed dish from The Rogue Gentlemen delivers. Nothing is expected, yet everything works together effortlessly—from the mackerel and miso-beet vinaigrette to the sweet mint and toasted pistachios.

INGREDIENTS

- ¼ C SALT
- 2 C WATER
- 1 MACKEREL FILET
- ½ C RED WINE VINEGAR
- ¼ C MIRIN
- 1 TSP SUGAR
- 4 MEDIUM BEETS
- 2 TSP VEGETABLE OIL
- 4 TBSP MISO AND BEET VINAIGRETTE (RECIPE PG. 195)
- 10 BABY SWISS CHARD OR BEET LEAVES
- 10 SWEET MINT LEAVES
- 10 BABY SORREL LEAVES
- ¼ C TOASTED PISTACHIOS
- SALT AND PEPPER, TO TASTE

INSTRUCTIONS

Pickle mackerel

1. Dissolve salt in water to make a brining solution. Place mackerel filet in brining solution for 3 hours, or until firm. Then thoroughly rinse fish in cold water.
2. Prepare a pickling liquid by mixing red wine vinegar, mirin, and sugar until sugar dissolves.
3. Cut mackerel filet on a bias into ½-inch strips. Then place fish slices in pickling liquid. Pickle for a minimum of 3 days.

Roast beets

1. Preheat oven to 400 degrees.
2. Coat beets in vegetable oil and season with salt and pepper. Place beets in a baking dish with enough water to cover the bottom of the pan.
3. Cover and bake until tender, approximately 45 minutes–1 hour.
4. Let cool and remove skins from beets with a towel. Cut beets into quarters and set aside 1 beet for the miso and beet vinaigrette, and the others for the salad.

Assemble salad

1. To plate, spread 1 tablespoon of vinaigrette in the center of 2 plates.
2. In a large bowl, toss roasted beets, Swiss chard or beet leaves, mint leaves, and baby sorrel leaves with 2 tablespoons of vinaigrette.
3. Portion salad onto each plate.
4. Sprinkle with toasted pistachios and arrange 5 pieces of pickled mackerel on each salad.

— THE ROGUE GENTLEMEN —

MISO AND BEET VINAIGRETTE

1 roasted beet, peeled and cut into quarters

2 Tbsp red miso

½ c rice wine vinegar

2 Tbsp sugar

1½ c grapeseed oil

Salt and pepper, to taste

Place beets in a blender with miso, rice wine vinegar, and sugar. Puree in blender at low speed.

Increase the speed of the blender and slowly add oil, ensuring the vinaigrette doesn't separate. If vinaigrette is too thick, add a little water to thin to desired consistency.

Season with salt and pepper to taste.

DOLORES PARK

YIELD: 1 COCKTAIL

This springtime cocktail features housemade falernum, a sweet syrup with notes of cloves, allspice, and nutmeg found in many Caribbean drinks.

INGREDIENTS

- 2 OZ CONTINENTAL GIN
- ¾ OZ FALERNUM (RECIPE ADJACENT)
- 1 OZ PINEAPPLE JUICE
- ½ OZ FRESH LEMON JUICE
- 1 BOTTLE LICKINGHOLE CREEK 'TIL SUNSET IPA (ONLY A FEW OUNCES ARE USED TO TOP OFF THE COCKTAIL)
- 1 SPRIG MINT

INSTRUCTIONS

1. Add gin, falernum, pineapple juice, and lemon juice to a cocktail shaker filled with ice. Shake vigorously for 20 seconds.
2. Strain into a Collins glass filled with ice.
3. Top with IPA.
4. Garnish with mint.

FALERNUM

- 25 cloves
- 20 allspice berries
- 1 whole nutmeg
- 375 ml Wray and Nephew White Overproof Rum
- Zest of 3½ limes
- ⅛ c ginger, peeled and medium diced
- ¾ c simple syrup (1:1 ratio of water to granulated sugar heated until sugar has dissolved)
- 1 tsp almond extract

Toast cloves, allspice, and nutmeg in a pan over medium-high heat until fragrant, about 4 minutes.

Combine rum, lime zest, ginger, and toasted spices in a plastic or glass container. Let infuse overnight.

Strain infused rum through cheesecloth. Whisk in simple syrup and almond extract. Store in bottles or capped containers in refrigerator.

L'OPOSSUM

SWEETBREADS
WITH LOBSTER
AND GRITS

FOIE GRAS
WITH
STRAWBERRY
AND
RHUBARB

HOT
BLACK
BOTTOM
À LA
MODE

L'Opossum may be a relative newcomer in the Richmond food scene, but it's a lifetime in the making for owner and chef David Shannon.

The colorful lights? David has collected them for years because they remind him of the living rooms of his childhood, full of shag carpet and chain lamps. The paintings that line the walls? Some came from thrift stores, others from respected artists, but they all spoke to him.

"Some people say it's too tacky, but others focus on how warm and elegant it is," he says. "People have a hard time describing what's happening here, which kind of means I'm doing it perfectly."

David applies that same personal touch to the menu, pulling from his decades of experience. After culinary school and a stint in New Orleans, he spent eight years at The Inn at Little Washington, where he started as an intern and left executive sous chef. He then returned to his hometown of Richmond, where he took over as the chef at Helen's before opening his first restaurant, Dogwood Grille and Spirits. He sold it in 2007 and stepped away from the industry, even considering other career paths.

But he never stopped looking and wondering what he would do if he got the chance to open another restaurant. When a space in Oregon Hill became available, David knew the timing was finally right.

His strong French background is certainly present at L'Opossum—staging at Abbaye de Sainte Croix and L'Oustau de Baumanière, two Michelin Star restaurants in France, continues to be an influence—but he doesn't take himself too seriously. Whether he's bringing in traditional Southern elements, such as the escargot served with a ham biscuit, or using local lore to describe an appetizer, the same quirky personality that added a letter and an apostrophe to "make an opossum fancy" is present in every line of his menu.

"I didn't want a serious French restaurant," he says. "You could play it off that way with the food that I serve. This keeps it fun and casual."

A few dishes, like the Hot Black Bottom À La Mode Topped by a Dominant Rich Ganache and Whipped Cream, even call back to that lifetime leading up to L'Opossum. David first made the popular Southern chocolate cupcakes as a child, using a recipe from a church cookbook. Today's version trades cream cheese for mascarpone and ditches the church picnic for a little naughtiness.

"It's really fun to create the whole experience and environment," he says. "It's more than just cooking somebody dinner. I was trying to think of what's current and what's going to be next, but in the back of my mind I was like, 'No, do it the way you want to do it. At least it will be different.'"

David Shannon

— L'OPOSSUM —

WHERE DO YOU GO OUT TO EAT?

Sally Bell's Kitchen, Chicken Fiesta, Fleurie in Charlottesville.

WHAT'S THE LAST MEAL YOU MADE FOR YOURSELF?

Caesar salad. I like to put different things on it. My favorite is bratwursts steamed in beer on top of a Caesar salad.

WHAT'S YOUR FAVORITE KITCHEN MUSIC?

Disco.

WHAT'S THE STRANGEST INGREDIENT YOU'VE EVER WORKED WITH?

When I was at the Inn at Little Washington, people used to come by the back door with things they had foraged. Usually it was wild mushrooms or asparagus. We had people that raised rabbits and occasionally people would show up with rattlesnakes that they had killed. You kind of sear it, then braise it.

WHAT WAS YOUR INTRODUCTION TO COOKING?

I had a great aunt who would sit for me and my brother when my parents would go out. She would always bake a cake or make something as a way of keeping us entertained. I was real little then, so I was mainly just watching. But it was just so cool that you had to take all of these different things and out would come a whole different new thing.

— L'OPOSSUM —

SWEETBREADS WITH LOBSTER AND GRITS

YIELD: 4 SERVINGS

David Shannon gives the classic shrimp and grits an upscale makeover. He replaces the shrimp with butter-poached lobster and throws in pan-seared sweetbreads for good measure. Creamy mascarpone and fragrant lavender jazz up the grits, and the dish is finished with a classic French lobster sauce—ironically called sauce Américaine.

INGREDIENTS

- 1½ C WATER
- 1 C WHITE WINE
- 1 LEMON, SLICED
- 1 ONION, ROUGHLY CHOPPED
- ½ CELERY RIB, ROUGHLY CHOPPED
- 1 BAY LEAF
- 2 CLOVES GARLIC, SMASHED
- 3 SPRIGS FRESH THYME
- 8 BLACK PEPPERCORNS
- 2 LBS SWEETBREADS
- 2 1¼-LB LOBSTERS
- 1 LB BUTTER
- ½ C ENGLISH PEAS
- 12 OZ HARICOTS VERTS
- KOSHER SALT, TO TASTE
- ¼ C VEGETABLE OIL
- 1 SPRIG TARRAGON

INSTRUCTIONS

Poach the sweetbreads

1. In a medium pot bring water, white wine, lemon, onion, celery, bay leaf, garlic, thyme, and peppercorns to a boil. Reduce to a simmer and cook for about 6 minutes. Strain, reserving the liquid; this liquid is referred to as court bouillon.

2. Bring court bouillon back to a gentle simmer and poach sweetbreads for about 10 minutes.

3. Place sweetbreads on a plate and top with a second plate that is weighted down. Press sweetbreads overnight in the refrigerator to remove excess liquid.

4. Once pressed, remove the membrane between sections and slice or pull sections apart into 3- to 4-ounce pieces.

Steam lobster

1. Place whole lobsters in a large steamer for 5–7 minutes. The meat will not be completely cooked at this point but will finish cooking when poached in butter.

2. Allow lobsters to cool completely, and then remove all the meat from the tails, claws, and knuckles. Reserve lobster shells to make the sauce.

CONTINUES ON NEXT PAGE

— L'OPOSSUM —

Butter poach lobster and vegetables

1. Melt butter in medium saucepan and bring to a gentle simmer. Add lobster meat, peas, and haricots verts and heat, just below a simmer, for 3–4 minutes.

2. Remove everything from butter and season with salt to taste.

Sauté sweetbreads

» In a heavy sauté pan, heat vegetable oil over medium-high heat. Sauté sweetbread pieces until they are a deep golden-brown, 2–3 minutes per side.

Assemble

1. Serve with mascarpone grits and sauce Américaine (recipes pg. 203).

2. Spoon grits onto center of 4 plates.

3. Top with lobster, vegetable mixture, and sweetbreads.

4. Spoon sauce around grits to cover the rest of the plate.

5. Garnish with fresh tarragon.

— L'OPOSSUM —

MASCARPONE GRITS

2 c whole milk

1 c heavy cream

2 Tbsp dried lavender flowers

1 c stone-ground grits

¼ c mascarpone cheese

Kosher salt and cayenne pepper, to taste

Combine milk, cream, and lavender flowers in a medium saucepan and bring to a gentle simmer.

Simmer for about 2 minutes, then remove from heat. Let milk steep for about 5 minutes, then strain, reserving liquid and discarding lavender.

Return the liquid to the saucepan and bring to a simmer. Mix in grits and cook for about 20 minutes, stirring frequently.

Once grits are tender, remove from heat and fold in mascarpone cheese. Season with salt and cayenne pepper to taste.

SAUCE AMÉRICAINE

¼ c vegetable oil

2 lobster body shells, coarsely chopped

1 c onion, chopped

½ c celery, chopped

½ c carrot, chopped

3 Tbsp tomato paste

3 sprigs fresh tarragon

2 bay leaves

1 Tbsp whole black peppercorns

2 c + 3 Tbsp dry sherry

1 qt heavy cream

Kosher salt, sugar, and cayenne pepper, to taste

Heat oil in a large saucepan over medium-high heat.

Add lobster shells, onion, celery, carrot, tomato paste, tarragon, bay leaves, and peppercorns. Cook for about 5 minutes.

Deglaze pan with 2 cups sherry. Light sherry on fire. Caution: Flames could be high; have a lid close by if needed. Simmer liquid until pan is almost dry.

Add cream and simmer until reduced by half and thickened.

Strain sauce and add 3 tablespoons sherry. Season with salt, sugar, and cayenne pepper to taste.

— L'OPOSSUM —

FOIE GRAS WITH STRAWBERRY AND RHUBARB

YIELD: 4 SERVINGS

At L'Opossum, we use fresh duck foie gras from the Hudson Valley in New York. It is available at specialty butchers, grocers, or online at D'Artagnan.

Foie gras is sometimes sold by the slice, but most often sold whole. Slices should be approximately 3 ounces per serving, and no less than ½-inch thick to sear to a medium rare. It is very difficult to properly cook a thin slice of foie gras.

Ingredients

- 1 PT VERY RIPE STRAWBERRIES + ¼ C FINELY DICED
- ¼ C SWEET ONION, DICED
- 1 THUMB-SIZE PIECE OF FRESH GINGER, PEELED AND DICED

- ⅓ C WHITE BALSAMIC VINEGAR
- ⅔ C WATER
- ½ C HONEY
- CAYENNE PEPPER, TO TASTE
- SUGAR, TO TASTE

- ⅛ C RHUBARB, FINELY DICED
- 2 TBSP SWEET WHITE WINE, SUCH AS SAUTERNES
- 1 MEDIUM RED ONION, SLICED ½-INCH THICK

- 12 ASPARAGUS SPEARS, BOTTOMS TRIMMED
- 3 TBSP OLIVE OIL
- 4 3-OZ SLICES FOIE GRAS, ½-INCH THICK

- 4 TSP PISTACHIOS, TOASTED AND ROUGHLY CHOPPED
- 2 TSP CHIVES, CHOPPED
- SALT AND PEPPER, TO TASTE

INSTRUCTIONS

Make strawberry sauce

1. In a large saucepan, combine 1 pint strawberries, sweet onion, ginger, white balsamic vinegar, water, and honey.

2. Bring to a simmer and cook until ingredients are very soft, 8–10 minutes.

3. Puree sauce in blender and strain through fine mesh sieve.

4. Season with salt and cayenne pepper to taste, and taste for sweetness. If you feel sauce isn't sweet enough, add up to a ½ tablespoon sugar. It should taste sweet, but balanced with vinegar. It should also have a hint of savory and the heat of the onion and cayenne. Set aside.

Make strawberry-rhubarb relish

1. In a small bowl, mix ¼ cup finely diced strawberries with rhubarb and white wine.

2. Season with salt and sugar to taste. When seasoning, keep in mind that salt is added to enhance flavors; you do not want to taste the salt in the relish.

— L'OPOSSUM —

Char onion and asparagus

1. Heat a grill or cast-iron skillet on very high heat.

2. Drizzle red onion slices and asparagus with olive oil and season with salt and pepper.

3. Cook onions and asparagus until slightly softened with some char, about 2 minutes for asparagus and 2 minutes per side for onion. This adds a smoky element to the dish. Set aside.

Sear foie gras

1. Preheat a large skillet or cast-iron pan over high heat. It is important that the pan is very hot when the foie gras is added. If the foie gras does not immediately sizzle and smoke, then the pan is not hot enough. There will be lots of smoke during cooking, so be sure to turn on your exhaust or open a window.

2. Season both sides of the foie gras with salt and pepper.

3. Add foie gras to hot pan and sear for about 30 seconds per side. It should have a deep brown color.

4. Remove from heat and let drain on a paper towel.

Assemble

1. Spoon 2 tablespoons of strawberry sauce in the center of 4 plates.

2. Layer a slice of charred onion, 3 asparagus spears, and a slice of foie gras over the sauce.

3. Garnish each plate with 1 tablespoon strawberry-rhubarb relish, 1 teaspoon pistachios, and ½ teaspoon chives. Serve immediately.

— L'OPOSSUM —

HOT BLACK BOTTOM À LA MODE

YIELD: 18 CAKES

Any good Southerner probably knows about black bottoms from church picnics and community cookbooks. The cupcakes were ingrained in David's youth—he's been making them since he was 10 years old—but here, Valrhona chocolate and mascarpone cheese take the recipe up a notch.

INGREDIENTS

8 OZ MASCARPONE OR CREAM CHEESE, SOFTENED

⅓ C + 1 C SUGAR

⅛ TSP + ½ TSP SALT

1 EGG

1 C SEMI-SWEET CHOCOLATE CHIPS, CHOPPED (VALRHONA PREFERRED)

1½ C ALL-PURPOSE FLOUR

¼ C COCOA POWDER (VALRHONA PREFERRED)

1 TSP BAKING SODA

1 C WATER

½ C CANOLA OIL

1 TBSP SHERRY VINEGAR

½ TBSP VANILLA EXTRACT

— L'OPOSSUM —
IN THE KITCHEN WITH DAVID SHANNON | HOT BLACK BOTTOMS

INSTRUCTIONS

1. Preheat oven to 350 degrees.
2. Cream together mascarpone, ⅓ cup sugar, and ⅛ teaspoon salt until smooth.
3. Add egg to cream cheese mixture and beat until smooth. Fold in chocolate chips.
4. In a large bowl, sift together flour, cocoa powder, baking soda, 1 cup sugar, and ½ teaspoon salt.
5. In a medium bowl, combine water, canola oil, sherry vinegar, and vanilla extract.
6. Add water mixture into flour mixture and beat until smooth.
7. Heavily spray cupcake pan or use cupcake liners. Fill each cup a little less than halfway with cake batter.
8. Drop a heaping tablespoon of the cream cheese mixture into the center of each cup.
9. Bake for 20 minutes. Remove from oven and let cool.

OPTIONAL GARNISHES:

Whipped cream, chocolate sauce, berries, and mint

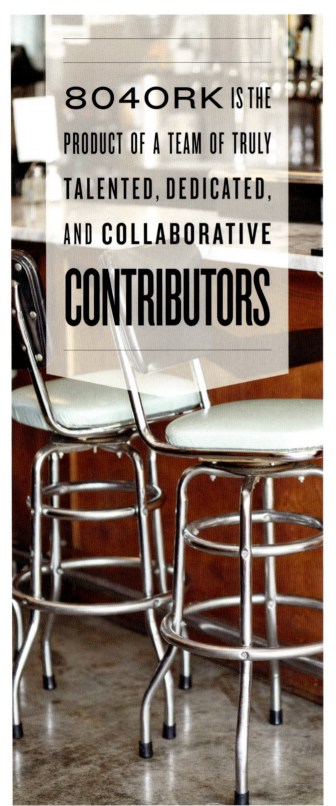

804ORK IS THE PRODUCT OF A TEAM OF TRULY TALENTED, DEDICATED, AND COLLABORATIVE CONTRIBUTORS

— THE PHOTOGRAPHERS —

CHRISTOPHILE KONSTAS
OPHILE.COM | PERKBONAIR.COM

shot photos for:
BOKA GRILL AND GROWLERS
THE CONTINENTAL WESTHAMPTON
CROAKER'S SPOT
SOUTHBOUND
TARRANT'S CAFÉ
THE URBAN TAVERN

After working for four years in forensic photography, Christophile Konstas went back to grad school in 2004 to study documentary filmmaking. Having grown up in a Greek family, with both parents in the food business, she recognized the intrinsic connection between food and culture and desired to tell those stories in her filmmaking. After moving back to Richmond in 2009, she collaborated with Nicole Lang to make *Pimento Cheese, Please!*, their first production for their soon-to-be-formed company, Pared Pictures.

Christophile lives with her husband and two sons on the southside of the river and is the co-owner of local coffee shop Perk! Bon Air.

WHAT ARE YOUR GO-TO INGREDIENTS?

My family's own EVOO from their olive orchards in Southern Greece. I swear by Kalas Sea salt, garlic, onions, oregano, lemon (just for me, the boys in my household don't care for lemons). And we always have flour tortillas and pupusa cheese around.

— THE PHOTOGRAPHERS —

MOLLY PETERSON
MOLLYMPETERSON.COM | HERITAGEHOLLOWFARMS.NET

photo by Mike Peterson

shot photos for:

THE DAILY KITCHEN AND BAR

GRAFFIATO RICHMOND

LUNCH. AND SUPPER!

PERLY'S RESTAURANT AND DELICATESSEN

Molly has been a professional photographer for over 10 years, from the mountains of Aspen to the Virginia Piedmont. As the director of photography for two regional food publications that celebrated local and sustainable food and farmers, she is a two-time finalist for the American Society of Magazine Editors' annual Best Cover award. Molly is known for her food and farm shoots, and has contributed to multiple cookbooks, which she finds amusing since she used to think pancakes came from a box.

She lives with her husband, a chef-turned-farmer, in Sperryville, Virginia, where they raise pasture-based livestock on nearly 600 acres of leased land at Heritage Hollow Farms.

WHAT'S YOUR FAVORITE DISH TO COOK FOR FAMILY AND FRIENDS?

Breakfast. I really love to put together a nice breakfast when folks come over: homemade biscuits, locally made jam, our farm's bacon or sausage, and eggs.

KIERAN WAGNER
KIERANWAGNER.COM

shot photos for:

DECO RISTORANTE

L'OPOSSUM

METZGER BAR & BUTCHERY

THE ROGUE GENTLEMEN

SAISON

In addition to being a photographer, Kieran is a lifelong musician and audio engineer. Educated at the Berklee College of Music, he spent years in famed New York and Miami recording studios before returning to Richmond to raise a family.

Kieran and his wife, Elissa, value the decidedly cosmopolitan bent of the city's growth over the last decade or so, especially as pertains to the restaurant scene. It's a little harder to miss Manhattan with such a fine crop of culinary talent right here in Richmond.

Kieran recalls that he bought a Holga out of nowhere in 2006, and lucky for us, he's been shooting ever since.

WHAT'S THE LAST MEAL YOU MADE FOR YOURSELF?

An invented sandwich: leftover grilled pork and thin-sliced roasted turkey ('cause I ran out of pork!) on a potato roll with a little Duke's mayonnaise, Le Grand tzatziki, bibb lettuce, pickled onions, salt and pepper, and some Mrs. Marshall's potato salad on the side.

— THE CREATIVE TEAM —

KIM CATLEY
KIMCATLEY.COM

Writer & Editor

responsible for:
CHEF INTERVIEWS
CHEF PROFILES
RECIPE INTRODUCTIONS
FINAL EDITING

Kim Catley loves good stories and good food, but especially when the two are shared with good people. For *804ork*, she was excited to tell the stories behind the places where these three things so often come together.

By day, Kim writes stories and words for all manner of things in the University of Richmond's communications office. She's also a yoga teacher at Project Yoga Richmond.

Kim lives in Bellevue with her husband, Daniel, and dog, Hattie.

WHAT WAS YOUR INTRODUCTION TO COOKING?

My grandfather's biscuits and mashed potatoes, my aunt's homemade pastas, and my grandmother's love of good restaurants.

WHAT'S YOUR FAVORITE COOKING MUSIC?

The Rolling Stones, Sharon Jones, the Wood Brothers, Steep Canyon Rangers, and Old Crow Medicine Show are often on repeat.

CHRIS GATEWOOD
THRESHOLD.CC

Writer & Legal Advisor

responsible for:
CHAPTER INTRODUCTIONS
INDEX
COPYRIGHT/ISBN
CONTRACTS

Chris is a lawyer who was once a reporter and doesn't mind a good side project once in a while. The concept for *804ork* dawned on him several years ago and he recruited help for the first volume in late 2012. Since then he has done a little bit of writing, a little bit of editing, and a lot of bit of help behind the scenes.

In his day job, Chris works with lots of startup companies, innovators, and intellectual property owners of all sizes at Threshold Counsel, the firm he started in 2010 after stints at large firms in D.C. and Richmond.

WHERE DO YOU GO OUT TO EAT?

The Magpie and The Roosevelt

WHAT'S YOUR FAVORITE COOKING MUSIC?

Americana and '90s rap

— THE CREATIVE TEAM —

MARCELLA LEE
BROADAPPETITE.COM

CARRIE WALTERS
CARRIEINK.COM | BLUNT-OBJECTS.COM

Food Editor & Photographer

responsible for:

RECIPE TESTING & EDITING

RECIPE INTRODUCTIONS

and shot photos for:

BOMBOLINI PASTA

THE DOG AND PIG SHOW

EARLY BIRD BISCUIT CO. & BAKERY

PIZZA TONIGHT

THE SAVORY GRAIN

SHORYUKEN RAMEN

ALL "IN THE KITCHEN" FEATURES

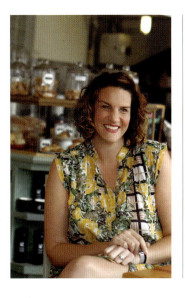

Creative Director, Publisher, & Editor

responsible for:

CONTENT CURATION

PROJECT MANAGEMENT

DESIGN & ILLUSTRATION

PUBLISHING

SALES & WHOLESALE DISTRIBUTION

Marcella is a recipe developer, food photographer, and most notably the voice behind the blog Broad Appetite. In 2014 she won *Saveur*'s Best New Food Blog award and has had recipes featured in *The Huffington Post*. She is an adventurous cook who is fascinated by how culture is expressed through food.

Besides food, she loves her fiancé, two dogs, and living in Church Hill.

WHAT'S THE LAST MEAL YOU MADE FOR YOURSELF?

Black Shin instant ramen topped with scallions, fried spam, kimchi and a poached egg. Korean ramen is one of the first foods I made myself and is straight-up comfort food. I eat it way too often.

WHAT'S THE STRANGEST INGREDIENT YOU'VE EVER WORKED WITH?

Vietnamese minced prawns. I won't lie—it looks scary. But it's shockingly good eaten right out of the tin.

Carrie spends her time developing brands for clients as Carrie, Ink and developing products as Blunt Objects. It was when she enlisted the help of Chris Gatewood to set up her companies that he approached her with a potential collaboration. For an avid cookbook ~~hoarder~~ collector, his idea was too tempting to pass up—and *804rk* was born.

When she's not working, Carrie likes to spend as much time as possible with her husband Matt, their ragtag crew of animals, and an occasional 2.5 tons books at their home in the country*.

*Also known as: "On the way to Charlottesville"; Proper name: Oilville, Virginia.

WHAT ARE YOUR GO-TO INGREDIENTS?

A menu. I can order food really, really well.

WHAT'S YOUR FAVORITE STUDIO MUSIC?

I run on a steady mix of KEXP, old-school hip-hop, and the occasional Icelandic electronic band—all really loud. Which is probably why my husband keeps buying me headphones.

— ACKNOWLEDGMENTS —

THANK YOU

I'd like to start by thanking every single one of you who bought, borrowed, flipped through, or even raised an eyebrow of approval at the original *804ork*. You made this book possible and for that I am truly grateful. I'm also extremely grateful to have landed in a city where a one-man shop can actually pull off a product like the one you're holding and have the support it needs to market and distribute right along with the big guys. As a community, our dedication to local products, services, and minds will only continue to make Richmond that much more amazing—and I feel lucky to be a part of such an encouraging environment.

Four years ago I got my very first wholesale order—and had no idea what I was doing. Thankfully Stan and Garnett at Mongrel have been there to answer all of my dumb questions, and to encourage me as I design new products and continue to grow this company. Over the past year I've met a handful of other local shopowners who have been just as amazing to work with: Anne, Jill, Anita, Ward, Erin, Carol, Scott, John—thank you! You make carrying around 40 pounds of books something I actually look forward to doing.

Back to that local talent. The main goal of this project is to properly show off the loaded pool of culinary genius in this town. Without all of you—the chefs and proprietors—there obviously wouldn't be an *804ork*, let alone a Volume 2. Your enthusiasm to participate in this project was infectious and humbling. I hope we did your food and your stories the justice they deserve.

I'd like to give a special thanks to Joe Sparatta, Lee Gregory, Kevin Roberts, and Tim Bereika for being so happy to work on a second book (even after my 9th and 20th annoying emails about recipes). You guys really are the best!

Christophile, Molly, and Kieran: You guys are the best team of photographers a girl could ever hope for. Your shots continue to take my breath away and you make my job a million times easier. Thank you for all of your hard work once again.

Kim and Marcella: You two are the real deal. This book would still be stuck in Evernote if it weren't for your enthusiasm and drive. Kim—your tenaciousness and ability to keep everything organized and on schedule made me inappropriately confess my love for you on more than one occasion. And I'm not sorry. Marcella—I'm so glad I tricked you into friendship at the Mid-Atlantic Food Writer's Symposium and get to collaborate with you on projects. Your talent is inspiring and I can't wait to see what you do next.

Chris: Thank you for always having my back, being my legal sounding board, and taking me on entrepreneurial adventures.

Laura Sant: You beautiful nerd—I'm so happy to have your words as the perfect start to this book. I know I'm not the only person who anxiously awaits the day you decide to make Richmond home again.

Janice, Katie, and Jennifer: Thank you for your support and coordination skills.

To everyone else who offered their help, but I ran out of either time or pages—don't worry. I'm sure by this point we're already working on something new. Robey, Nick, Mattias—I'm talking to you.

And finally, I want to thank everyone's families for being so patient and understanding over the past six months. Lee, Daniel, Tommy, Matt—you all deserve a night out on me. (We can even invite Chris, Kim and Marcella if you want!) I also want to thank my Mom and Dad for single-handedly convincing every person living in the Manakin-Sabot ZIP code that they needed a cookbook. Let's hope they're ready for round two.

I could probably go on for at least two more pages thanking everyone—plus I haven't even begun my odes to cold brew, Stella's Grocery, or my dog Marco—but you get the point. This project is a beast and it takes the blood, sweat, and tears (oh yes, there are tears) of many special people to make it all come together. So to sum it up I'll simply say—thank you all!

Carrie Walters

804RK · CONTRIBUTORS · PAGE 215 EARLY BIRD BISCUIT CO. & BAKERY SHOT BY MARCELLA LEE

— DIRECTORY —

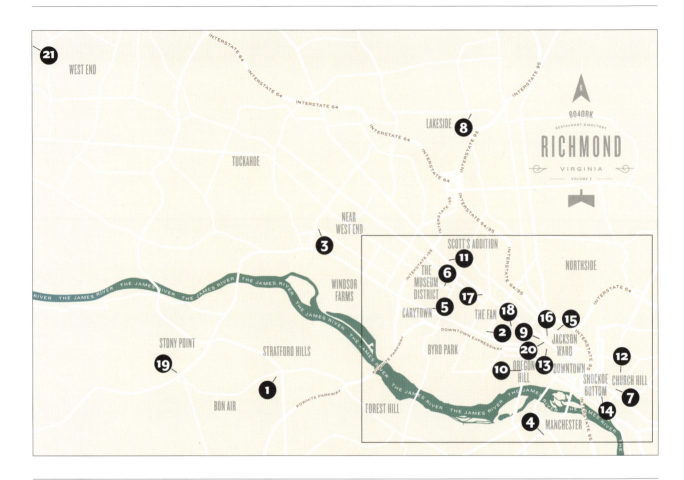

DIRECTORY

4
CROAKER'S SPOT
1020 HULL ST.
RICHMOND, VA 23224
(804) 269-0464
croakersspot.com

6
DECO RISTORANTE
2901 PARK AVE.
RICHMOND, VA 23221
(804) 342-4278
decorichmond.com

8
EARLY BIRD BISCUIT CO. & BAKERY
5411 LAKESIDE AVE.
RICHMOND, VA 23228
(804) 335-4570
earlybirdbiscuit.com

1
BOKA GRILL AND GROWLERS
2557 SHEILA LANE
RICHMOND, VA 23225
(804) 928-2652
bokatruck.com/bokagrill

2
BOMBOLINI PASTA
1606 W MAIN ST.
RICHMOND, VA 23220
(804) 213-0212
bombolinipasta.com

3
THE CONTINENTAL WESTHAMPTON
5704 GROVE AVE.
RICHMOND, VA 23226
(804) 285-0911
thecontinentalrva.com

5
THE DAILY KITCHEN AND BAR
2934 W CARY ST.
RICHMOND, VA 23221
(804) 342-8990
thedailykitchenandbar.com

7
THE DOG AND PIG SHOW
314 N 25TH ST.
RICHMOND, VA 23223
(804) 303-5958
thedogandpigshow.com

9
GRAFFIATO RICHMOND
123 W BROAD ST.
RICHMOND, VA 23220
(804) 918-9454
graffiatorva.com

804RK · DIRECTORY · PAGE 216

— DIRECTORY —

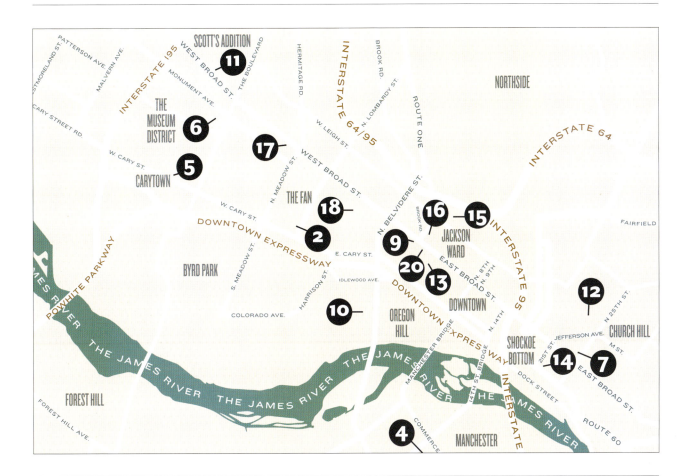

L'OPOSSUM
626 CHINA ST.
RICHMOND, VA 23220
(804) 918-6028
lopossum.com

METZGER BAR & BUTCHERY
801 N 23RD ST.
RICHMOND, VA 23223
(804) 325-3147
metzgerbarandbutchery.com

PIZZA TONIGHT
2110 E MAIN ST.
RICHMOND, VA 23223
(804) 658-4968
pizzatonight.com

SAISON
23 W MARSHALL ST.
RICHMOND, VA 23220
(804) 269-3689
saisonrva.com

SHORYUKEN RAMEN
900 W FRANKLIN ST.
RICHMOND, VA 23220
(804) 855-4246
shoryukenramen.com

TARRANT'S CAFE
1 W BROAD ST.
RICHMOND, VA 23220
(804) 225-0035
tarrantscaferva.com

LUNCH. AND SUPPER!
1213–1215 SUMMIT AVE.
RICHMOND, VA 23230
(804) 353-0111
lunchorsupper.com

PERLY'S RESTAURANT AND DELICATESSEN
111 E GRACE ST.
RICHMOND, VA 23219
(804) 332-6434
fb.me/perlysrichmond

THE ROGUE GENTLEMEN
618 N 1ST ST.
RICHMOND, VA 23219
(804) 477-3456
theroguegentlemen.com

THE SAVORY GRAIN
2043 W BROAD ST.
RICHMOND, VA 23220
(804) 592-4000
thesavorygrain.com

SOUTHBOUND
3036 STONY POINT RD.
RICHMOND, VA 23235
(804) 918-5431
southboundrva.com

THE URBAN TAVERN
10498 RIDGEFIELD PKWY.
HENRICO, VA 23233
(804) 716-7028
theurbantavern.com

— INDEX —

EARLY BIRD BISCUIT CO. & BAKERY SHOT BY MARCELLA LEE

INDEX

— A —

Almond Chutney 174

Almond Horns. 123

Américaine, Sauce 203

Anderson, Brittanny 136–138

Asparagus. 186

Avocado Puree 183

— B —

Bacon Parmesan
    Brussels Sprouts 109

Baller Status 135

Bamboo Shoots,
    Marinated 34

Bayer, Jay 154

Beer-Brined Pork Chops 140

Bereika, Tim 178–180

Biscuits with Molasses
    Butter 19

Blackened Mahi Tacos 71

Blackening Seasoning. 73

Bohdan, Jami 46–48

Boka Grill and Growlers 58

Bombolini Pasta 10

— C —

Caramel, Salted, Sauce 91

Carbonara, Bucatini 131

Carbonara, Fettuccini. 14

Cauliflower Soup 174

Cauliflower, Roasted,
    with Brown Butter,
    Capers, and Pistachio
    Gremolata. 185

Chicken 162

Chorizo 95, 161

Bread Pudding 44, 105

Bread Pudding,
    Coconut Raisin with
    Whiskey Sauce 44

Bread Pudding,
    Sweet Potato. 105

Brown Sugar Bay Leaf
    Ice Cream 145

Bruschetta, Wild
    Mushroom 74

Bruschetta Tomatoes. 51

Brussels Sprouts 77, 109

Burrata with Tomato,
    Corn, Arugula, and
    Country Bread 130

Chorizo Pâté. 161

Cilantro-Lime Emulsion 73

Cocktails 135, 197

Coconut Raisin
    Bread Pudding with
    Whiskey Sauce 44

Coconut-Habanero Broth. 158

Continental Steak Sauce 89

Continental
    Westhampton, The. 82

Crab 42, 52, 110

Crab Imperial Dip 110

Crème Brûlée,
    Café Mocha 67

Crispy Skin Red Snapper 63

Crispy Stuffed Squash
    Blossoms 52

Croaker's Spot 98

— D —

Daily Kitchen and
    Bar, The 68

Deco Ristorante. 146

DeRoche, Victoria 23–24

Dog and Pig Show, The 92

Dolores Park. 197

Duck Confit with Fava
    Beans, Artichokes,
    Morels, Fennel, and
    Carrot-Chèvre Puree. 191

— E —

Early Bird Biscuit Co.
    & Bakery 16

Eckrosh, James and
    Isabel 93–94

Eggleston III, Neverett 98

— F —

Falernum. 197

Fettuccini Carbonara 14

Fettuccini, Fresh. 13

Fig 26, 61, 62

Fig and Pig Pizza. 26

Fig-Ginger Compote 62

Fish 41, 63, 71, 100, 103,
    112, 139, 171, 182, 194

Flautas, Fig and Pig 61

Foie Gras with Strawberry
    and Rhubarb. 204

From the Creek to
    the Cabin. 112

— INDEX —

— G —

Golden, Jared 68
Graffiato Richmond 126
Grape, Smoked,
    Salad 65
Gregory, Lee 166
Grits 51, 112, 203
Grits, Mascarpone 203
Grits, Stone-Ground
    Gouda 51

— H —

Hall, Adam 154–156
Harris, Patrick 58–60
Hash, Sweet Potato
    and Chorizo 95
Herb Vinaigrette 65
Hiyashi Chuka 32
Hiyashi Dressing 34
Hot Black Bottom
    à la Mode 206
Housemade Marinara 86

— I —

Ice Cream 145
Insalata di Finocchi 151
Isabella, Mike 127–128

— K —

Kreckman, John 11–12
Kugel with Almond
    and Sunflower Crust 119

— L —

L'Opossum 198
Laxton, Tim 16–18
Lobster .201
Lowrie, Stuart 83–84
Lunch. and Supper! 106
Lyons, Rick 106–108

— M —

Mackerel, Pickled with
    Beets, Sorrel, Miso
    and Beet Vinaigrette,
    Pistachio, and Mint 194

Maher, John 189–190
Marinade, Peruvian 163
Marinara, Housemade 86
Marinated Bamboo
    Shoots 34
Mascarpone Grits 203
Maymont Afternoon 135
Metzger Bar
    & Butchery 136
Mint Pea Crème
    Fraîche 53
Miso and Beet
    Vinaigrette 195
Molasses Butter 19
Moon, Enjoli 98–99
Murphy, Sean 46–48
Mushrooms,
    Quick-Pickled 34
Mustard Seeds,
    Pickled 171

— O —

Onions, Fried 88

— P —

Parsnip Puree 57
Pasta 13, 14, 131, 152, 176
Pasta Trinacria 152
Pasta, Fresh, with
    Braised Short Ribs 176
Perly's Restaurant
    and Delicatessen 114
Peruvian Marinade 163
Peruvian Roast Chicken 162
Pickled Daikon Radish 34
Pickled Mustard Seeds 171
Pickled Red
    Cabbage Slaw 73
Pico de Gallo 73
Pig and Fig Flautas 61
Piquillo Bouillabaisse 65
Pizza 26
Pizza Tonight 22
Pork Chops, Beer Brined 141
Potato Crisps 65
Preserved Lemon
    Vinaigrette 122, 183
Prosciutto Cheese Sticks 85

— INDEX —

— Q —

Quick-Pickled
  Mushrooms 34

— R —

Rabbit Pot Pie 55

Radish, Pickled Daikon. 34

Ramen. 32

Red Cabbage Slaw,
  Pickled 73

Red Wine Vinaigrette. 130

Ribeye, Grilled,
  Housemade Steak
  Sauce, Fried Onions 88

Richardson, Will 28–31

Risotto-Style Farro with
  Asparagus, Oyster
  Mushrooms, and
  Parmesan. 186

Roberts, Kevin and
  Rachelle 114–116

Robinett, Matt. 127, 128

Rockfish, Pan-Seared 41

Rogue Gentlemen, The 188

Rundown .157

— S —

Saison 154

Salad: Insalata di
  Finocchi 151

Salmon 100, 171, 182

Salmon Chelsea. 100

Salmon Tartare,
  Avocado, Coriander,
  and Preserved Lemon
  Vinaigrette. 182

Salmon, Pastrami-Cured. 171

Salted Caramel Sauce 91

Santarella, Ted. 38–40

Sauce Américaine 203

Savory Grain, The 46

Scafidi, Giuseppe 147–148

Seafood Chili 103

Shannon, David. 199–200

She-Crab Soup 42

Shoryuken Ramen 28

Shrimp and Grits 49

Smoked Grape Salad 65

Smoked Trout Rillettes 139

Soup. 42, 174

Southbound. 166

Sparatta, Joe. 166–168

Spätzle. 141

Steak (Ribeye) 88

Steak Sauce, Continental 89

Sticky Toffee Pudding 91

Stone-Ground Gouda
  Grits 51

Sweet Pea Mash 57

Sweet Potato and
  Chorizo Hash 95

Sweet Potato Bread
  Pudding 105

Sweetbreads with
  Lobster and Grits. 201

— T —

Tacos, Blackened Mahi 71

Tarrant's Café. 38

Tempura Batter 86

Toffee Pudding,
  Sticky 90

Trout, Smoked,
  Rillettes 139

— U —

Urban Tavern, The 178

— V —

Veal Schnitzel
  Perlstein. 121

Veggie Burger. 78

Vinaigrette, Herb 65

Vinaigrette,
  Miso and Beet 195

Vinaigrette,
  Preserved Lemon. 122, 183

Vinaigrette,
  Red Wine. 130

— W —

Wallof, Ted. 68

Wild Mushroom
  Bruschetta. 74

Williams, Michelle. 68–70

THE CONTINENTAL WESTHAMPTON SHOT BY CHRISTOPHILE KONSTAS